Fashion

Brimming with creative inspiration, how-to projects and useful information to enrich your everyday life, Quarto Knows is a favourite destination for those pursuing their interests and passions. Visit our site and dig deeper with our books into your area of interest: Quarto Creates, Quarto Cooks, Quarto Homes, Quarto Lives, Quarto Drives, Quarto Explores, Quarto Gifts, or Quarto Kids.

First published in 2018 by Aurum Press, an imprint of The Quarto Group. The Old Brewery, 6 Blundell Street, London N7 9BH, United Kingdom. www.QuartoKnows.com

A catalogue record for this book is available from the British Library.

ISBN 978 1 78131 695 5

10 9 8 7 6 5 4 3 2 1
2021 2020 2019 2018 2017

Design by ascopedesign
with a2creative design, Kei Ishimaru and binomi design
Typeset in Neutraface 2, Playlist and Butler Stencil
Printed in China by C&C Offset Printing Co., Ltd.

Karen Homer

Fashion

THE ESSENTIAL VISUAL GUIDE TO THE WORLD OF STYLE

10

CHAPTER 1
MATERIALS
& PRINTS

34

CHAPTER 2
CLOTHING TRENDS
& STYLES

60

CHAPTER 3
THE FASHION
INDUSTRY

102

CHAPTER 4
FASHION
ERAS

132

CHAPTER 5
THE BODY
BEAUTIFUL

158

CHAPTER 6
ACCESSORIES,
FOOTWEAR & JEWELLERY

FOR HOWARD, OLLIE AND KITTY

INTRODUCTION

Fashion is first and foremost a visual medium: the delicate hue of a wispy chiffon dress; the elaborate embroidered detailing on a pair of couture shoes, or the deep, weathered patina of a vintage leather bag, these are things we appreciate sensually, so surely the best way to present information about fashion is also via appealing graphics. This is especially true in a world where we are used to the instant visual gratification of Snapchat and Instagram, with little time or inclination to read lengthy features, even on subjects we love.

This book does just that, offering a wealth of bite-sized information including facts and figures about aspects of the fashion and accessories industries, behind-the-scenes looks at fashion shows and magazine shoots, and details of the mechanics of clothes production. If you have ever wondered how designers choose their colours for the next season, how long it takes to get a hot new look copied from the catwalk to the high street, or even the number of hours it takes to create an haute couture dress, the information is right here. If you are into retro or vintage there are pages devoted to eras gone by, snapshots of how the biggest fashion icons created their statement looks and, in a world where pretty much anything goes style-wise, you can choose your favourite from round-ups of the many versions of clothes and accessories including dresses, skirts, coats and hats.

When I first started writing about fashion, almost twenty years ago, things were very different; everything was pinned on the 'big four' shows – New York, London, Milan and Paris – and there was no knowing what designers had created if you didn't have a coveted ticket to the hottest shows. Fashion lovers waited with baited breath for the essential September and March issues of the top fashion magazines in order to find out what they should be wearing, and it was worth investing in designer clothes because high-street stores couldn't compete. Today shows are live-streamed via the internet and brands like Zara get their copies into stores within two to four weeks, far sooner than the designers themselves can manage. Fashion bloggers, uploading content and pictures from the ground, have more influence than fashion editors who have spent decades in the business, leading to public conflict in some memorable cases.

Today fashion is fast, in every sense of the word, but that comes with a downside, as fast fashion often means disposable fashion, which brings us to the dark underbelly of the industry: the poorly paid labourers working in unsafe conditions in developing countries and the masses of unwanted clothes piling into landfill across the globe. Fortunately, sustainable fashion has become increasingly popular, with big brands signing on to ethical production with a demand for transparency about their manufacturing practices, widespread recycling of clothes and a movement towards upcycling and repurposing unwanted clothes.

The face of fashion has also started to change for the better, with an increasingly diverse portfolio of models featured in mainstream fashion editorials. It is refreshing to see models of all ages, ethnicities, body shapes and genders beginning to be more fairly represented.

On a less serious note, fashion should be about self-expression and fun, and this book offers something for everyone. From the extreme body art that is such a part of many people's looks to the trend for designer-fashion-clad dogs, this book will hopefully expand what fashion means to you, make you think about what has gone before and perhaps inspire you to try something new. After all, as Marie Antoinette's dress designer Rose Bertin is said to have stated, 'There is nothing new except what has been forgotten!'

CHAPTER 1

MATERIALS & PRINTS

Everything we think of as 'fashion' starts with fabric; from soft natural wools to slippery synthetics, every garment needs to be created using exactly the right cloth, which in turn dictates the movement of the dress, the cling of the sweater or the structure of a jacket. And beyond cloth there is colour and print, where textile designers and dye specialists have only the limits of their imaginations to create patterns and shapes that give us the vast array of choice that we take for granted when we choose what to wear. This chapter looks at how different fabrics are created, from egalitarian cloths like denim to highly sought-after artisan products such as Harris Tweed, as well as examining patterns and prints that have become iconic. Lastly, with such choice comes responsibility and with the wealth of material available, how we shop ethically and produce clothes sustainably, and how we care for our clothes to ensure their longevity, are important questions to ask ourselves as lovers of fashion.

CUT FROM DIFFERENT CLOTHS

Fabric for clothes is made from more than you think – wood pulp, pineapple, worm cocoons, nettle leaves and glass are all used in the manufacture of fabric and textiles. Fashion has never been shy of experimenting with the weird and the wonderful. Animal textiles, once the main fabric used in clothing, are now less popular, in part thanks to animal rights activists. Even plant textiles can raise sustainability issues, meaning that manufacturers are working hard to create synthetic textiles that have the appearance and qualities of natural fibres.

SYNTHETIC TEXTILES

Rayon, viscose, modal and acetate, designed to mimic expensive silk, are technically natural in origin but have been manufactured using heavy chemical processes. Nylon, the first synthetic fibre, created in 1938, is essentially a plastic but was marketed as a new wonder-fabric and will forever be remembered for creating a hosiery revolution. Polyester is hugely successful in the creation of durable, quick-drying and wrinkle-resistant clothing, and is now gaining environmental approval as it can be created using recycled plastic bottles. Acrylic can be spun to resemble wool or cotton and is often used as a synthetic alternative to wool. Spandex, Lycra and elastane contain at least 85 per cent polyurethane, enabling fibres to be stretched to almost 500 per cent. They are popular in sportswear and stretch-denim.

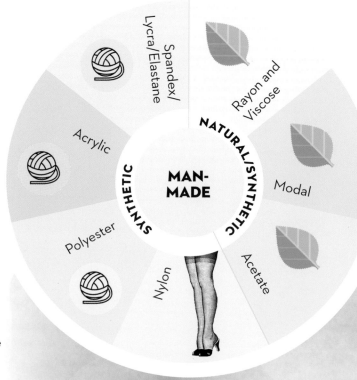

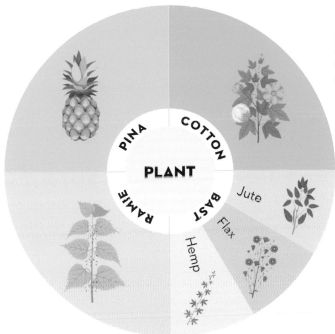

PLANT TEXTILES

Cotton, made from the soft, white fibres that surround the seed of the cotton plant, is a versatile and breathable natural fibre used in many types of clothing. Bast fibres are strong cellulose-based fibres from plants including jute, flax and hemp. The degree of processing dictates the qualities of the end fabric, for example both hessian (rough and open in weave) and linen (fine and soft) are woven from the flax plant, with very different results. A natural fibre called ramie is derived from a plant in the nettle family. It is relatively weak, so often mixed with cotton or other fibres. Pina is a fibre derived from the leaves of the pineapple plant.

ANIMAL TEXTILES

Animal furs have been used to make clothes since primitive man first needed extra warmth. Similarly, leather from tanned animal skins has a long history in the fashion industry. Wool is the most common animal hair used, while the finest type of animal textile is made from the cocoons of silkworms.

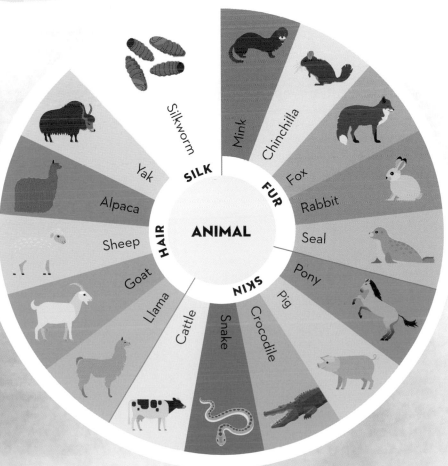

TO DYE FOR

The first synthetic dye was invented in 1856 by a young chemist named William Henry Perkin. Perkin was trying to find a synthetic source of quinine – then the only cure for malaria – when he realised the coal-tar solution he was testing dyed his test strip purple. Further experiments revealed that this colour, which he called 'mauve', was not only far denser than previously used natural dyes, but also did not fade in sunlight. Thus the first chemical dye was born. Today, it is estimated that more than 10,000 different dyes and pigments are used in industrial dyeing. However, the downside to this has been environmental pollution, as well as health risks to workers who are often inadequately protected against the harmful chemicals.

HOW TO NATURALLY DYE FABRIC

Transforming the colour of your clothes using natural dyes is surprisingly simple if you follow the right steps.

1. MAKE THE DYE

Place several handfuls of the dye source, such as plant leaves, roots (finely chopped) or berries and herbs, in a large pot that you do not mind staining. Add double the quantity of water to plant material. Simmer for an hour, strain the liquid, then return it to the pot.

2. FIX THE FABRIC

For the dye to 'take', the fabric needs to be prepared with a fixative. Berries require a salt fixative of half a cup of salt to eight cups of water. Plants use a vinegar fixative of one part vinegar to four parts water. Boil the fabric in the fixative for one hour, then rinse thoroughly.

3. DYE THE FABRIC

Place the fabric in the dye pot and simmer until you achieve the required colour density. For a strong shade, let the fabric soak overnight after boiling. Remember that the fabric will appear darker when wet, and larger amounts of fabric require more dye.

4. WASH THE FABRIC

Remove the fabric, rinse thoroughly and leave to dry. Always wash dyed fabric separately or with like colours and keep in mind that natural dyes will fade with exposure to sunlight and washing.

SOURCES OF NATURAL DYES

A vast rainbow of colours can be extracted from natural sources, including fruits, berries, herbs and roots.

YELLOWS
Bay leaf, marigold, sunflower, St John's wort, dandelion, paprika, turmeric, celery leaf, lilac twig, saffron, sassafras bark, mahonia root, barberries

ORANGES
Carrot, gold lichen, onion skin, alder bark, bloodroot, giant coreopsis, sassafras leaf

BROWNS
Dandelion root, oak bark, walnut hull, tea, coffee, acorn

RED & BROWNS
Pomegranate, beetroot, bamboo, hibiscus, bloodroot, eucalyptus bark, madder root, sumac fruit, dandelion root, blackberries

PINKS
Raspberries, strawberries, cherries, red and pink rose, avocado skin and seeds, grand fir bark

RED & PURPLES
Sumac berries, purple basil, day lily, pokeweed berries, huckleberries, purple or red lichen

GREYS & BLACKS
Iris root, sumac leaf, black walnut, oak gall

BLUES & PURPLES
Indigo, woad, red cabbage, elderberries, red mulberries, blueberries, purple grapes, dogwood bark, red cedar root

GREENS
Artichoke, sorrel root, spinach, peppermint leaf, snapdragon, lilac, grass, nettle, plantain, peach leaf, eucalyptus leaf, camellia, foxglove, tea tree, yarrow

GOING GREEN

In recent years, more and more fashion brands
promoting ethical business practices have come to
the fore. By promising fair pay for their labour forces
and drastic reductions in carbon emissions and waste,
these companies are working to find a balance between
affordable fashion and ethical manufacturing conditions.
The rise of super-cheap clothing, though a bonus for the
high street, has thrown behind-the-scenes cost-saving
methods into sharp focus, prompting forward-thinking
brands to guarantee a renewable, sustainable production
process. The only really effective way to minimise the
impact of our fashion choices, however, is to buy
fewer clothes, which means less fast fashion.

We own four times
as many clothes now
as in 1980

In the United States, eight-five per cent of the
twenty-five billion pounds of textiles generated
each year goes to landfill

ETHICAL FASHION

- ⚲ FAT FACE
- ⚲ EILEEN FISHER
- ⚲ PEOPLE TREE
- ⚲ ASOS ECO EDIT
- ⚲ H&M CONSCIOUS
- ⚲ TOPSHOP RECLAIM
- 🍃 NISOLO SHOES
- ⚲ PATAGONIA
- 🍃 EVERLANE

GRAPHIC KEY:

- ⚲ **Sustainable fair trade fashion brands**
- 🍃 **Green initiatives**

🍃 **Sustainable Clothing Action Plan** Reducing carbon, water and waste emissions worldwide.

🍃 **Better Cotton Initiative** Fighting for workers' rights and sustainable growing and production practices worldwide.

🍃 **Circular Fashion** Launched by Swedish firm Green Strategy, a closed-loop production model where the end product is broken down into its component parts and recycled into a new version of itself.

£140

million worth of clothing goes to landfill each year in the UK

UPCYCLED FASHION

We are a disposable society and nowhere more so than with our clothes. We own four times as many clothes as we did in 1980 and, while we are getting better at donating, recycling and repurposing, there is still a lot more to be done. In the UK, thirty per cent of the average wardrobe hasn't been worn in over a year.

WHAT WE THROW AWAY AND WHERE IT GOES

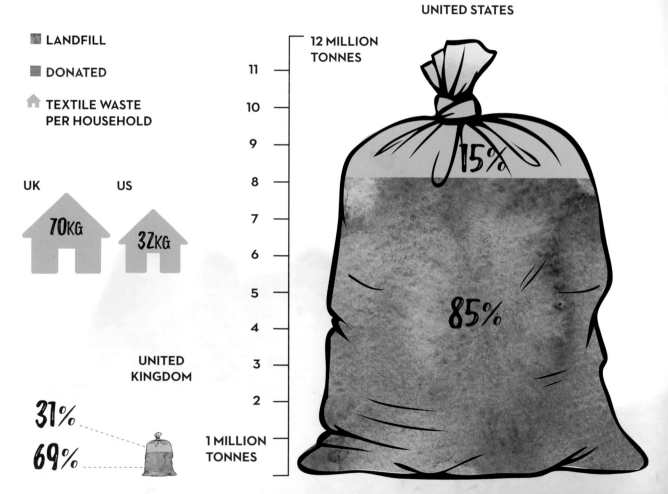

LANDFILL

DONATED

TEXTILE WASTE PER HOUSEHOLD

UK
70KG

US
32KG

UNITED STATES

12 MILLION TONNES

15%

85%

UNITED KINGDOM

31%
69%

1 MILLION TONNES

VALUE OF EXPORTED USED CLOTHING (MILLIONS)

While a proportion of donated clothes will be distributed by local or national charities or resold in charity shops, a large amount is exported each year to be sold for profit overseas.

UNITED STATES — $687

UNITED KINGDOM — $612

GERMANY — $504

SOUTH KOREA — $364

NETHERLANDS — $236

BELGIUM — $189

CANADA — $185

POLAND — $141

ITALY — $141

JAPAN — $120

MAKE DO AND MEND

Give jeans, jackets and sweaters new life with patches.

Make 'sweater mittens' or hats by repurposing the sleeves of old jumpers.

Use various old pieces of fabric to make quilts or rag-rugs.

Re-dye faded clothes with a washing-machine dye or reinvent with a natural dye (see pages 14–15 for how to do this).

Learn to knit, crochet, sew and darn.

Take any unwanted items to stores that offer recycling services, such as:
- H&M
- Patagonia
- North Face
- Eileen Fisher
- Levi's
- Marks & Spencer
- Uniqlo

TRUE BLUE

A hard-wearing fabric that transcends class, wealth and status, denim's origins can be traced back to the hardy trousers worn by the sailors of Genoa in sixteenth-century Italy. The word denim is thought to be a bastardisation of 'de Nîmes', the town of Nîmes in France being a source of the cloth. Levi Strauss is credited with the invention of jeans as we know them; in the 1850s, he created an industrial-strength labourer's cloth held together by copper rivets. Once James Dean appeared in a pair in the 1955 film *Rebel Without a Cause*, they hit the fashion mainstream, with women's jeans catching up fast thanks to Marilyn Monroe's love of the indigo cloth.

STONEWASHED DENIM

A bleached denim created by putting stones in an industrial washer to give the jeans a worn, mottled look.

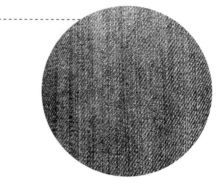

WAXED DENIM

Adding a thin wax coating to classic denim is a trick designers sometimes to use to give these smarter jeans a luminescent quality.

TWISTED DENIM

The yarn of the cloth is over-twisted, giving the finished jeans a crinkled appearance.

SELVEDGE

Thicker, darker and stiffer than other varieties, this is seen as a more sophisticated denim.

STRETCH DENIM

A varying mix of cotton with man-made fibres and elastane makes for a forgiving jean, often worn super-skinny.

RAW DENIM

This is denim that has not been pre-washed in the factory, a common practice to avoid shrinkage when washing.

ACID-WASH DENIM

Jeans bleached with stones soaked in a chlorine solution for a uneven mix of pale and dark shades.

DENIM BY NUMBERS

100

Number of layers of denim which are stacked together and weighted down to keep them in place whilst the pieces are cut.

15

Pieces of denim to make up the standard pattern for a five-pocket pair of jeans.

6

Stonewashing takes between 30 minutes up to 6 hours of washing and 1kg of pumice stones per pair to achieve a more or less faded finish.

1.6

Each pair of jeans takes 1.6 metres of fabric, several hundred metres of thread, 6 rivets, up to 5 buttons, 4 labels and an optional zip.

15

The minutes it takes to put together one pair of jeans.

WOVEN HERITAGE

Islanders on the Outer Hebrides off the coast of Scotland had been weaving the sturdy woollen cloth that became known as Harris Tweed for centuries when, in the 1840s, Catherine Murray, Countess of Dunmore, started to promote the cloth amongst her aristocratic friends. The countess sent two local sisters to mainland Scotland for formal weaving tuition; on their return the women shared their knowledge with local weavers and the Harris Tweed industry was born. Always associated with the highest quality of raw materials and hand-craftsmanship, the reputation of Harris Tweed grew so great that in the early twentieth century it became necessary to stamp the cloth with a newly registered Trade Mark of the Harris Tweed Association Ltd to protect its authenticity. The 'Orb' trade mark is still stamped on every bolt of cloth to this day, but Harris tweed is no longer the preserve of the aristocracy – it has become the cloth of choice for international designers and celebrities and is found not only on clothes, but on products as diverse as iPhone cases and upholstery covers. The quality is still unsurpassed.

THE PROCESS OF MAKING TWEED

1 STAMPING

Before a piece of cloth can receive the famous 'Orb' trade mark of Harris Tweed, it must be examined thoroughly by the independent Harris Tweed Authority. The stamp is ironed onto the reverse of the fabric.

2 GATHERING THE WOOL

The pure virgin wool that will become Harris Tweed comes from sheep from the Scottish mainland and island sheep that are rounded up and shorn by locals.

3 WASHING & DYEING

Unlike much other wool, the wool for Harris Tweed is dyed before it is spun, which means different natural hues can be carefully blended prior to dyeing to create subtle shades.

4 BLENDING & CARDING

Before spinning the wool, the white and coloured yarn is weighed then carefully blended. Next, the fibres are teased apart, cleaned, straightened and mixed.

5 SPINNING

The fragile carded yarn is twisted as it is spun to give the wool strength. The spun yarn is wound on to bobbins providing for both weft (left-to-right threads) and warp (vertical threads).

6 WARPING

The warp threads are gathered together in a specific order on a warping frame so the colour pattern of the finished cloth is accurate. This essential part of the process was at one time done by hand.

7 WEAVING

According to the Harris Tweed Act of 1993, all Harris Tweed has to be woven in the home of one of the islanders of the Outer Hebrides. The bobbins of wool are delivered to be woven on a treadle loom.

8 FINISHING

The greasy woven wool, which still contains the oil used to dye it, returns to the mill where darners inspect it closely to correct any imperfections before it is thoroughly washed and beaten, then dried, steamed, pressed and cropped.

IN PRINT

Among the vast array of fabric prints are various iconic patterns that stand out, often worn by people who have a sure sense of their own personal style, regardless of what is in fashion.

GEOMETRIC
A variety of bold shapes, often with a 1960s feel, can instantly make a fashion statement.

PINSTRIPE
Classically used in menswear for suiting fabric, but adopted by women wanting an androgynous look. Often light stripes on a dark background, but they can be any colour.

BRETON STRIPE
Based on the French naval seaman's uniform of 21 stripes – one for each of Napoleon Bonaparte's victories – the classic pattern was popularised by Coco Chanel in 1917.

PLAID/TWEED
A hand-woven fabric originally used by Scottish and Irish farmers to protect themselves from the cold. Tweed became popular when Estate tweeds were created to mark individual clans, worn by both noblemen and their workers.

POLKA DOT
Named after the polka music of the mid-nineteenth century, this pattern has been forever imbued with elegance thanks to Christian Dior's love of the polka dot in his New Look collection of the 1950s; it is a vintage classic.

PAISLEY
Though it can be traced back to 50 BC Persia, the pattern was first recorded on fabric on sixteenth-century Kashmir shawls. Shawl-making later spread to Europe, with the largest production site in Scotland, hence the pattern's British name.

HOUNDSTOOTH/ DOGSTOOTH
Originating in Scotland in the 1800s, and traditionally worn by shepherds, two-tone houndstooth is made of abstract four-pointed shapes, often in black and white, and is most often used on wool or tweed.

ARGYLE
Derived from the seventeenth-century tartan of the Campbell Clan of Argyll in Scotland and taken up by Pringle after the First World War, argyle often appears on socks or sweaters, and is popular among preppy men, golfers and Japanese fashion aficionados.

GINGHAM
Derived from the Malay-Indonesian word *genggang*, meaning striped, the checked cloth made its way to Europe in the early seventeenth century, taking off during the Industrial Revolution when cloth production in Manchester's cotton mills made it popular.

IKAT
This ancient technique, traditionally produced in Indonesia and other parts of Asia, as well as Africa and South America, creates its distinctive pattern by tie-dyeing threads on a frame before weaving, resulting in an imperfect print with fuzzy, overlapping edges.

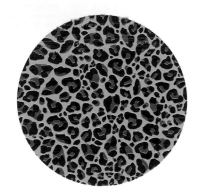

LEOPARD PRINT
Animal skins were always an indicator of status, but in the 1920s glamorous movie stars adopted the print. Popular throughout the twentieth century, animal print has a risqué connotation and is variously seen as trashy, downmarket or high fashion.

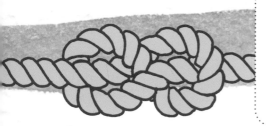

JEAN SEBERG
The 1960 film *Breathless* saw the star of French New Wave cinema in a Breton stripe and casual rolled-up jeans, exuding free love.

BRIGITTE BARDOT
The French actress exudes sex appeal in any outfit including her wardrobe staple, a Breton top.

JAMES DEAN
With his trademark cool, the actor wore a v-neck, collared Breton top in the 1955 movie *Rebel Without a Cause*.

COCO CHANEL
The woman who started the trend, Coco Chanel matched her Breton top with wide-leg trousers for a look that was revolutionary in 1917.

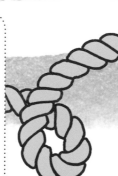

JEAN-PAUL GAULTIER
The bad-boy French designer is an ambassador of the Breton stripe, in his own wardrobe, on the catwalk and in his high-street range for Target, Australia.

NAUTICAL CHIC

The iconic striped Breton top first appeared in 1858 as the uniform for French naval seamen from Bretagne, hence the name. The design originally featured 21 stripes, one for each of Napoleon Bonaparte's victories. It became a style classic when Coco Chanel, inspired by the sailors she saw, included the striped top in her nautical-themed collection of 1917. To this day, the Breton top is a versatile piece that works within an enormous variety of styles, from classically elegant to high fashion.

AUDREY HEPBURN

In the 1957 film *Funny Face* and off-screen, the stylish actress often paired a Breton top with cropped trousers for her trademark casual style.

KATE MOSS

The supermodel wears her stripes under everything, including leather, fur and designer jackets.

THE DUCHESS OF CAMBRIDGE

Classic to the end, the Duchess teams her stripes with a fitted blazer and skinny trousers.

ALEXA CHUNG

The model and presenter adores classic stripes, wearing them regularly with denim skirts, jeans or tucked into leather shorts.

PABLO PICASSO

Many iconic photographs of the painter capture him in his trademark Breton tops.

OLIVIA PALERMO

Unafraid to glam up her stripes with a miniskirt, heels and designer handbag, this it-girl is often papped wearing the iconic style.

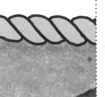

A LIFE IN STYLE AUDREY HEPBURN

There are few women for whom the epithet 'icon of style' really applies, but Audrey Hepburn is one. Despite, or perhaps because of, her own admission that she never thought of herself that way, her simple, gamine style has endured to this day. Whether barefoot dressed in black leggings and a striped Breton top or draped in jewels wearing the most perfectly crafted little black dress of all time, Hepburn never failed to encapsulate what it means to be chic.

ROMAN HOLIDAY

Hepburn shot to fame in the 1953 film *Roman Holiday* and the image endures of her joyfully dashing about Rome on the back of Gregory Peck's scooter dressed in a full skirt, white shirt and neck scarf, finished off with a pair of strappy sandals. Chic and innocent, it is a fresh summer look, forever associated with the actress's style.

SABRINA

The 1954 film *Sabrina* was the first time designer Givenchy dressed the actress who would become his muse, although it was the Paramount studio's costume designer Edith Head who walked away with an Oscar for the film. The glamorous black and white ball gown with it's ornate embroidery and dramatic train was Oscar-worthy in itself, and the black cocktail dress with it's tiny waist and straight 'boat' neckline sparked such a trend it became known as the 'Sabrina' neckline. Extremely flattering, Audrey fell in love with this neckline that hid the bony collarbones she felt self-conscious about, while accentuating her shoulders.

1 FUNNY FACE

Trained as a ballerina, Hepburn perfectly suited the all-black, gamine dancer's skinny cropped trousers and black top worn by her character in the 1957 film *Funny Face*. Behind the scenes her cropped black trousers were often paired with a classic striped Breton top as the actress waited in rehearsals.

2 BREAKFAST AT TIFFANY'S

The most iconic of all Hepburn's dresses is the black Givenchy shift dress she wore as Holly Golightly in *Breakfast at Tiffany's*. Sold for a record-breaking £467,200 at auction in 2016, this particular version might be the ultimate black dress, but Hepburn wore many black shift dresses, often accessorised with pearls and a scarf or sunglasses and an oversized hat.

3 CHARADE

Incognito or not, Hepburn was often seen in a classic belted trench coat, complemented by a headscarf and oversized glasses – worn on-screen in *Breakfast at Tiffany's* and her 1963 film *Charade* with co-star Cary Grant, as well as off-screen when eluding the fans and paparazzi.

COLOUR CRAZY

If you've ever wondered who determines which colour is going to be 'in' next season, meet the colour forecaster: part fortune-teller, part researcher, the colour forecaster will know what you are going to be wearing two years before you do. Researchers tap into global trends not only in fashion but also interiors, environment and politics, trying to capture the cultural zeitgeist and project its hues. Biannual meetings at Pantone, the American company that maintains colour standards across a range of industries, invite colour projectors, textiles representatives and fashion brands to debate the merits of colour families, divine which colours will be the ones to capture fashion designers' and the public's imagination next, and painstakingly narrow down a core group from Pantone's overwhelming range of close to 2,000 shades. The result isn't quite a diktat, but it certainly nudges the fashion world in the direction of a particular palette, sending the message that green... or orange... or yellow... is 'the new black'. In fact, each year Pantone names a 'colour of the year', some of which are represented here.

PANTONE
15-4020
Cerulean

PANTONE
17-2031
Fuchsia Rose

PANTONE
13-1106
Sand Dollar

PANTONE
19-1557
Chili Pepper

PANTONE
17-1463
Tangerine Tango

PANTONE
17-5641
Emerald

2002
PANTONE®
19-1664
True Red

2003
PANTONE®
14-4811
Aqua Sky

2004
PANTONE®
17-1456
Tigerlily

2005
PANTONE®
15-5217
Blue Turquoise

2008
PANTONE®
18-3943
Blue Iris

2009
PANTONE®
14-0846
Mimosa

2010
PANTONE®
15-5519
Turquoise

2011
PANTONE®
18-2120
Honeysuckle

2014
PANTONE®
18-3224
Radiant Orchid

2015
PANTONE®
18-1438
Marsala

2016
PANTONE®
13-1520
Rose Quartz

PANTONE®
15-3919
Serenity

2017
PANTONE®
15-0343
Greenery

ALWAYS READ THE LABEL

Caring for your clothes should be easy,
but that little label inside your new dress has
a load of indecipherable symbols that mean if
something goes wrong and you haven't followed the
care instructions you will lose your statutory
right to return the garment, so here is what
all those squiggles actually mean.

HOW TO WASH DELICATES

Bra labels often say they should be hand-washed, but who has the time to do that? Nevertheless, it's a mistake to put your underwired bra loose in a washing machine as it can get tangled around other washing or the wire can come out and break the machine. Instead put bras inside a pillowcase or invest in a bra-washing net.

WASHING

Normal cotton wash at the temperature indicated

Wash using synthetics setting at the temperature indicated

Wash using wool setting at the temperature indicated

Hand-wash only

BLEACHING

Suitable for all clothes bleaches

Oxygen-based (non-chlorine) bleaches only

TUMBLE-DRYING

Can be tumble-dried

Tumble-dry on cool setting

Tumble-dry on hot setting

IRONING

Iron on cool setting

Iron on warm setting

Iron on hot setting

DRY-CLEANING

Can be dry-cleaned

Must be dry-cleaned using a specific process

Must be professionally wet-cleaned

DO NOT

Do not wash

Do not bleach

Do not tumble-dry

Do not iron

Do not dry-clean

CHAPTER 2

CLOTHING TRENDS & STYLES

Never before has there been such choice in the clothes we can wear to express our sense of style, whether you choose iconic classics or take a more maverick approach to fashion. This chapter looks both at traditional garment types and examines the vast array of styles within each genre, as well as the way in which fashion boundaries are being pushed. In addition, it examines the trend for men to follow their own fashion tribes and looks at new areas that have recently exploded within the fashion world, for example designer fashion for children.

DRESS TO IMPRESS

Legendary American *Vogue* editor Diana Vreeland once said, 'It's not about the dress you wear but the life you lead in that dress.' A good dress allows you to slip it on and forget about what you're wearing, getting on with your life knowing you look good. Luckily, there are shapes of dress for every body, style, age and budget.

SHIFT
Often sleeveless with a simple round neck, falling to the knee. A classic.

COCKTAIL
Knee-length and fitted, often a version of the little black dress.

TEA
Vintage-style day dress, made from a printed light fabric such as chiffon.

SHIRT
A dress version of a man's shirt falling to the knee, with sleeves of varying length.

EVENING
Formal, long gown suitable for smart occasions, with various necklines including strapless, off-the-shoulder or asymmetrical.

MAXI

Enduringly associated with the 1970s: long and voluminous, either in a bohemian print or more recently as a popular strapless summer wear.

MINI

Classic 1960s style: short or sometimes super-short dress in a simple design.

BODY-CON

Aka the bandage or bandeau dress, usually short and always super-fitted, this style of dress hides nothing.

A-LINE

A flattering style, popular both in the 1950s and 1960s; fitted at the bust or waist and flared in the skirt.

WRAP

A draped, tied-at-the-waist dress emphasising curves, often in a silk jersey and suitable for all occasions.

LITTLE BLACK DRESS

Black once signified mourning, but in 1919 fashion designer Coco Chanel denounced the colours of the dresses worn by the women at a charity ball she attended as 'too awful, they make the women ugly. I think they ought to be dressed in black'. And so the cult of the Little Black Dress (LBD) was born.

Modern LBDs take in classic shifts, halter-necks, asymmetrical and one-shoulder cuts, and flared prom-style numbers, many of which are based on these timeless designs.

THE DIOR LBD

Christian Dior's 'New Look' LBD emphasised an hourglass figure: cinched in at the waist, full and flared in the skirt, and cut into a deep V at the neck. An elegant mid-calf length gives this dress ballerina-like poise.

THE CHANEL LBD

Coco Chanel created the modern LBD when her design, dubbed 'Chanel's Ford' – as it was said to be as much of a design classic as the car – was featured in *Vogue* in 1926. The epitome of simple elegance, this dress is iconic 1920s Chanel: no restrictive corseting, a dropped waist, length on the knee, and perfectly accessorised with pearls.

THE MOVIE-STAR LBD

Cut on the bias, made from slinky satin-backed crêpe, this style is pure movie-star glamour. The body-skimming cut and revealing décolletage are in striking contrast to the more modest 1920s versions.

THE HEPBURN LBD

Think Audrey Hepburn starring in *Breakfast at Tiffany's* and wearing the most iconic LBD of all time, designed by Hubert Givenchy (see page 29). Long and sensuous, revealing the actress's delicate shoulders, this is a look that has been copied the world over.

THE 'REVENGE' LBD

Princess Diana's so-called 'revenge dress' epitomises the 1990s LBD. Diana made the decision to wear the cleavage-revealing, mid-thigh-length fitted black dress by Greek designer Christina Stambolian to an engagement on the same night that a television documentary aired revealing her husband, Prince Charles's, adulterous affair with Camilla Parker Bowles. The effect was sensational.

A LIFE IN STYLE
VICTORIA BECKHAM

Whatever your opinion on Victoria Beckham, there is no doubt that the former Posh Spice is brilliant at reinventing her image. Her metamorphosis over two decades from pop star, through footballer's wife, to become an understated and stylish, internationally-acclaimed fashion designer – and, don't forget, mother of four – is nothing short of spectacular. There are few women who can pull off such a transformation.

1 POP PRINCESS

Aged twenty-two, Victoria Adams shot to fame in iconic girl band the Spice Girls. She was dubbed 'Posh Spice' on account of her little black dresses, love of fashion and 'posh' pout. With a background as a model and dancer, Victoria favoured skimpy super-tight outfits, often appearing on stage in little more than a bra top and miniskirt.

WIFE & MOTHER

On 4 July 1999, Victoria married footballer David Beckham in a princess-like Vera Wang wedding dress, the stuff of every little girl's dream. With Victoria's hair newly cropped and spiked, baby Brooklyn in her arms as ring bearer, and a photoshoot in *Hello!* magazine, the couple had truly arrived.

WAG

As one of the footballers' 'wives and girlfriends', Victoria kept things true to form, accompanying David in short shorts and garishly coloured low-cut tops. A permanent suntan and streaked, tousled hair completed the look. In 2007 she appeared almost exclusively in body-con bandage dresses, mostly in bright colours or animal prints.

2 DESIGNER

For her 2008 appearance as a guest judge on US fashion reality show *Project Runway* Victoria pulled off a style transformation in a sophisticated orange drape dress. In the same year she launched her first fashion designs: a capsule collection of ten pared-down dresses that, despite the sceptics, was well received.

3 EVENING WEAR

Victoria has always loved fashion and in 2000 appeared on the catwalk for designer Maria Grachvogel. Before launching her own line, Victoria favoured glamorous designers for celebrity events such as Dolce & Gabbana, Roberto Cavalli and Roland Mouret, accessorised with fur stoles, plenty of jewellery and, as always, killer heels.

BUSINESS ICON

With the launch of Victoria by Victoria Beckham, a second lower-priced, more casual line, the designer won best brand at the 2011 British Fashion Awards and the clothes from her own label revealed a confident, stylish fashion designer and businesswoman. As her eponymous label goes from strength to strength, Victoria Beckham has cemented her place among the highest echelons of fashion.

SKIRTING THE ISSUE

Skirts are a fashion staple that have been in vogue for centuries – quite literally: in 2011 archaeologists in Armenia discovered fragments of a reed skirt dating from 5,900 years ago. Until Coco Chanel daringly started to wear men's trousers in the 1920s, women were expected to wear skirts or dresses. In fact, despite no one obeying it, it took until 2013 for a nineteenth-century French law that made it illegal for women to wear trousers to finally be repealed. It might be nearly a century since women started wearing trousers but the novelty wore off a long time ago and skirts are as in demand as ever. No one shape is in fashion and there are plenty of styles to choose from.

PENCIL
The elegant knee-length tailored skirt beloved of secretaries and 1950s ladies. Remains an office staple and classic vintage look.

MINI
Ranging from mid-thigh length to barely longer than a belt, either straight or slightly flared, this is for those who dare to bare all.

BUBBLE OR PUFFBALL SKIRT
The 1980s classic is often labelled as fashion's worst faux pas, yet they still appear!

TULIP
Like the flower, this design has an overlapping petal-like front and an oval shape. Most often falls to just on the knee.

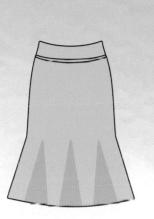

GODET SKIRT

A type of pleated skirt that has triangular inserts of fabric, or 'godets', inserted between the seams near the hem giving it volume and flare.

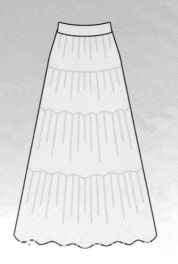

GYPSY SKIRT

A layered type of maxi skirt; team with an off-the-shoulder broderie anglaise blouse for nostalgic 1980s style.

MAXI

Bohemian hippies of the 1960s and 1970s wore these long skirts over hot pants. Now designs tend to be more subdued in print and worn with a fitted or crop top to balance the silhouette.

CIRCLE

A very full, flared skirt in varying lengths named for the pattern, which appears as a large circle. Shorter versions are pure rock-and-roll style.

A-LINE

Often with box pleats and falling to the knee, this is a flattering shape typical of the 1950s.

TULLE SKIRT

The full, frilly ballerina's skirt has made its way off the practice barre and on to the high street.

CAPE

A cape with armholes is a popular alternative to a coat, with an elegant vintage vibe.

DUFFLE

Also known as a 'toggle' coat, this hooded style is made from heavyweight woollen fabric that originated in the town of Duffel in Belgium. Classically lined in tartan fabric.

CROMBIE

Named after John Crombie, a Scottish early nineteenth-century cloth producer, this is a tailored single-breasted three-quarter-length coat made from fine wool fabric.

BABY, IT'S COLD OUTSIDE

Coats are not just about keeping warm; they are often the only part of an outfit on show, which is why there is a coat for all seasons and all styles.

FUR AND SHEEPSKIN

Despite protests from animal rights campaigners, fur, sheepskin and shearling coats are still popular. Vintage or faux fur are great options for the ethically minded and increasingly adopted by high-fashion trendsetters such as Stella McCartney.

WRAP COAT

As it sounds: a coat that wraps around and ties at the waist rather than buttoning.

PEA COAT

Invented by the Dutch in the 1800s and popularised by the British and later the American Navy, this double-breasted coarse-wool short coat is a popular classic.

SWING COAT

Originating in the 1950s when the fashion was for full coats with wide sleeves, this style is tailored to the waist with a swinging skirt.

TRENCH

The classic trench coat is a beige knee- or mid-calf length lightweight coat made from gaberdine, a unique rainproof fabric developed by Thomas Burberry in 1879.

PARKA

A military-issue coat adopted by the mods as streetwear in the 1960s, the parka, with its fur-lined hood and numerous cargo-pockets, is a utilitarian classic.

PUFFER

Originally designed by Eddie Bauer in the 1930s as a warm alternative to woollen coats, the down-filled, quilted design keeps wind out and distributes warmth evenly.

THE JACKET

A jacket can change an outfit in an instant and is the perfect trans-seasonal solution. There is a wealth of styles to choose from; here are some perennial favourites.

WAXED JACKET

Similar in style to the field jacket (see below), but in a unique waxed cotton. Developed by Barbour in the late 1800s it has long been associated with British aristocrats and country lifestyles. High-end waxed motorcycle jackets in cotton or leather are beloved of riders and celebrities.

FIELD JACKET

Known as the M65, this military jacket, beloved of Bob Marley and grunge kids everywhere, is usually olive green, with poppered pockets and a hood that rolls into the collar.

BLAZER

Single or double-breasted, with gold buttons or plain, in colours or tweed, there are endless variations on this tailored jacket.

BOLERO

Inspired by the matador, this very short cropped jacket with curved lapels is often worn over a dress for smart evening wear.

BOMBER JACKET

The original leather flying jacket was adopted by women in the 1950s, including Marilyn Monroe who paired the blouson jacket with her trademark tight dresses. Much used by Hollywood, fashion also has a love affair with the bomber, from the ubiquitous high-street version to embroidered and satin designs on the catwalk.

BIKER JACKET

The zipped leather motorcycle jacket first appeared in 1928 and was sold by a Harley-Davidson supplier. It was immediately adopted by a generation of bikers. Since then, Marlon Brando, James Dean, Sid Vicious and Bruce Springsteen have been linked to the jacket which, like other originally male styles, quickly became popular with women, too.

DENIM JACKET

As popular as jeans themselves, the denim jacket has been a fashion mainstay since the 1950s. Styles through the decades have ranged from dark blue and fitted to oversized and acid-washed, with embellishments including artwork, slogans, crystals and embroidery.

TUXEDO

Women's versions of the classic men's tux, black and longer-length with satin-covered lapels, are a statement alternative to glamorous dresses.

VARSITY

The all-American college letterman jacket has a contrasting coloured body and sleeves and often striped cuffs and hem.

CHANEL

While few can afford a genuine Chanel jacket, high-quality versions of the collarless fine-tweed jacket with its piped edge and contrasting colourways, are the ultimate in upmarket style.

GAME, SET & MATCH

'Athleisure' may be a recently coined term for the explosion in athletic brands that cross over as everyday wear, but the trend for comfortable, stylish activewear has been around for a lot longer.

For the first time, clothes are designed specifically for women to play sports such as golf and tennis. With the mass production of women's clothing after the First World War, this quickly turns into leisurewear.

1920s

In New York, several designers, among them Clare Potter and Claire McCardell (hailed as 'America's greatest sportswear designer'), create innovative designs for comfortable clothes in practical fabrics such as cotton and jersey.

1930s–1940s

Mostly female American designers continue to reject the corseted fashions coming out of Paris, instead experimenting with a more liberated fashion style, including relaxed pantsuits, trousers and activewear outfits with co-ordinating separates, a fundamental building block of sportswear design.

1950s

The heyday of the tracksuit: flared in the leg and tight in the body, jacket and trouser bearing a vertical stripe from chin to toe. Worn by footballers, school kids and break-dancers alike.

1970s

Hip-hop artists wear branded, oversized sportswear; shell suits are the ultimate in rave cool, and designer labels like Ralph Lauren and Tommy Hilfiger are emblazoned across tracksuits and hoodies. The trend for aerobics clothes as streetwear grows with the launch of brands like Sweaty Betty and Lululemon Athletica.

1980s–1990s

Stella McCartney designs Team GB's kit for the 2012 London Olympics and works with Adidas to create StellaSport. Pop collaborations hit the high street with Beyoncé's Ivy Park range for Topshop, Kanye West's Yeezy trainers with Adidas and Rihanna's Fenty Puma. Sports stars Serena Williams and Roger Federer become style icons.

2000s–2010s

MALE FASHION TRIBES

Since journalist Mark Simpson coined the term 'metrosexual' in 1994 to define a generation of high-disposable-income, globe-trotting men with a keen interest in fashion and personal grooming, men have been divided into style tribes. It's not just women who have to worry about what their clothing says about them any more.

LUXE SPORTSWEAR
Think hip-hop artists wearing high-fashion streetwear.

Statement jackets or sweaters

Jeans or sweatpants

Trainers

METROSEXUAL
The original fashion-conscious male, unafraid of his feminine side and originally epitomised by the likes of David Beckham.

Well-cut button-down shirts

Immaculately tailored suits and jackets

Big-brand labels

HIGH-FASHION ROCKER
Pop stars like Harry Styles embody the neo-rocker look.

Printed sweaters and sharp tailored coats, preferably by Yves Saint Laurent

Skinny, often ripped jeans

Chelsea boots or fashion trainers

TOUGH GUY
Jason Statham is the ultimate ambassador for tough guy style.

Shaved or semi-shaved head

V-neck or wool jumper

Belstaff-style jacket (but not too bikery)

Distressed jeans

Leather boots

MODERN HIPSTER
Also known as a 'lumbersexual' thanks to his penchant for lumberjack style.

Full and carefully groomed beard

Checked shirts or long t-shirts

Denim

Workboots

MODERN PREPSTER
A twist on the Americana look, the modern version of preppy style is less straight Ivy League than before.

Button-down shirts

Chinos or jeans, ironically rolled up

Deck shoes or desert boots

Reversed snapback baseball caps and beanies

Ankle-skimming chinos or baggy shorts, often with knee-high socks

Long layered tops or board-sport branded t-shirts beneath checked shirts or hoodies

VANS trainers

SKATER STYLE
Originating in 1970s California, skater style is going stronger than ever.

ANNA DELLO RUSSO
FASHION MANIAC

The editor-at-large for Japanese *Vogue* was once described by Helmut Newton as a 'fashion maniac'. She is certainly an eye-popping sight at fashion shows with her love of fruit-shaped headwear, garish prints, voluminous furry creations and outfits with a sci-fi influence.

MAVERICK FASHION

Maverick fashion designers and exhibitionist celebrities have pushed the boundaries of fashion throughout the decades, often rivalling one another to create outfits that are the most bizarre and outlandish. This is extreme fashion, designed to shock.

ALEXANDER MCQUEEN
BOUNDARY PUSHER

This British designer probably did more to push the boundaries of fashion than any other. His creations didn't just use incredible fabrics of all kinds, but featured startling materials. Such creations included fibreglass helmets, balsa-wood capes, potentially lethal glass corsets, animal horns and breastplates made from leather, plaster of Paris and perspex.

LADY GAGA
CHAMELEON SONGSTRESS
Lady Gaga's craziest outfits to date
have included appearing dressed like a
yeti, sporting beetle wings, wearing warrior-
maiden breastplates and, most infamously,
wearing a dress made from raw beef
at the 2010 MTV Video Music Awards.

ISABELLA BLOW
HAT QUEEN
Stylist, mentor to Alexander McQueen
and all-round eccentric, Isabella Blow loved
outlandish fashion. Hats were her trademark,
and she claimed that they were far more effective
at battling low moods than antidepressants. As
muse to iconic milliner Philip Treacy, she wore
sculptural headgear in the shape of a galleon
ship, a lobster and an oversized red perspex
disc that entirely covered her face.

HUSSEIN CHALAYAN
AVANT-GARDE DESIGNER
Chalayan collaborated with
Icelandic singer Björk in the 1990s and
hit the headlines in a 2000 show when
he featured models stepping into
pieces of furniture, which then
became part of their outfits.

MADONNA
MATERIAL GIRL
In her decades-long career Madonna
has worn underwear as outerwear, rubber,
leather and plenty of iron hardware and
outfits with religious undertones. Her most
shocking outfits featured Jean-Paul Gaultier's
revealing corsetry, with trademark
conical bras, or a bondage-style
corset with no bra at all.

CRACK THE CODE

There are fewer events these days that specify the type of dress men and women are expected to wear, which makes it all the more important to get it right when the occasion arises.

MEN	DRESS CODES	WOMEN
• White bow tie • White waistcoat • Full tail coat • Optional: medals	**WHITE TIE** The most formal of dress codes, white tie means full evening dress and is usually reserved for state occasions.	• Evening gown, usually floor-length • Optional: tiara, elbow-length gloves
• Morning coat with tails • Black or grey-stripe trousers • Waistcoat • Tie • Optional: top hat	**MORNING DRESS** Otherwise known as 'formal day dress', this dress code is suitable for any event starting before 6 p.m., such as weddings, horse-racing and formal daytime events.	• Smart day dress, never above the knee • Jacket • Optional: hat
• Morning coat with tails • Black or grey-stripe trousers • Waistcoat • Tie • Optional: top hat	**BLACK TIE** Recently under this dress code men have started wearing long black neck ties rather than bow ties, although – from an etiquette point of view – this isn't strictly correct.	• Smart day dress, never above the knee • Jacket • Optional: hat
• Ordinary suit	**LOUNGE SUITS** A catch-all dress code for modern occasions, as many men these days don't possess a dinner jacket.	• Smart dress
• Suit • Tie, although you might get away without one	**COCKTAIL** For women, a classic cocktail dress is fitted and falls to below the knee; however the code encompasses all kinds of party dresses.	• Cocktail dress

DRESS CODES IN BUSINESS

CASUAL/DRESS DOWN
Men: jeans, t-shirt,
sweater, trainers
Women: jeans, casual skirt or
dress, t-shirt, sweater

BUSINESS CASUAL
Men: shirt with collar, khakis
or corduroy trousers, sweater,
casual shoes
Women: shirt or smart top, skirt
or trousers, casual shoes

SMART CASUAL
Men: smarter trousers, jacket,
dress shirt, tailored sweater, tie,
leather shoes
Women: smarter skirt, dress
or trousers, smart top or shirt,
leather shoes or boots

SMART
Men: suit, dress shirt, tie, formal
shoes. Optional: braces
Women: suit dress or skirt/
trouser suit, dress shirt, tights,
leather shoes

HERE COMES THE BRIDE

The wedding-dress market is a lucrative one, with couture gowns costing tens of thousands of pounds. Over the decades, wedding dresses have been just as much influenced by fashion as any other clothes, which is why looking back on the photos of your big day might make you cringe as well as smile.

Flapper-style, above the ankle, ornately embroidered dresses worn with cloche hats or Juliet headdresses were a world apart from the tightly laced bodices, bustles and layers of full skirts of the previous decades. The more streamlined silhouette was offset by huge bouquets.

1920s

Fabric rationing during and after the Second World War meant that wedding dresses had to be shorter, although the government did issue 200 coupons for a girl's special day. Even Queen Elizabeth had to use clothing coupons for her dress, which was made using silk from Chinese, rather than enemy Japanese, silkworms and 10,000 pearls from the United States.

1940s

1840

Queen Victoria set the precedent for white wedding gowns when she married Prince Albert on 10 February in the Chapel Royal at St James's Palace. Before this, white was seen as rather daring and only for the super-wealthy. The Queen chose her lace-covered gown not for its connotations of purity, but because she wanted to showcase the fine lace she loved while boosting a flagging industry.

1930s

The Great Depression meant less money for extravagance and many brides relied on hand-me-downs. Nevertheless, the wealthy embraced the glamour of the era. The advent of man-made fabrics like rayon offered cheaper alternatives and suited the slinky bias-cut styles of the decade.

1950s

The classic heart-shaped low-cut bodice, with a risqué exposure of the neck and shoulders, appeared in the 1950s. This was combined with a tiny waist and a full, calf-length skirt. Dress lines were much cleaner and elegantly simple, without the puffy sleeves or over-full skirts of the past.

Minidresses, pastel colours and big veils (for the more traditional) were all fashionable options in the 1960s. For her 1969 wedding to Italian Andrea Dotti, style icon Audrey Hepburn wore a classically sixties short, pale pink dress with matching headscarf.

In 1981 Lady Diana Spencer wore the dress that would outshine all others; made from ivory silk taffeta and antique lace adorned with sequins, beads, 10,000 pearls and a 25-foot train, it was pure eighties excess. The first haute couture wedding dresses paraded down the Chanel catwalk in 1987, taking the wedding dress to the next level of luxury and expense.

The choice of wedding dress attire in the twenty-first century is huge, from vintage dresses, white tuxedos, nude and sequinned cut-out gowns to the ever-popular classic 'bridal shape' exemplified by the gown designed for Catherine Middleton by Sarah Burton at Alexander McQueen.

1960s

1980s

2000s

1970s

1990s

The 1970s wedding dress was unstructured, with gypsy ruffled skirts and off-the-shoulder bodices, accessorised by floral crowns and long flowing tresses. Those less inclined to hippy-chic might choose a simple straight dress with a high neck and relatively little adornment.

Minimalism was key in the 1990s, with classic, elegant shapes taking precedence over bouffant concoctions. The 1996 marriage of Carolyn Bessette, wearing a simple slip dress, to John F. Kennedy Jr, is a perfect example.

MINI ME

Children, especially those belonging to celebrities, are no longer just offspring, but extensions of their parents' style, which goes a long way to explaining the explosion in designer and high-street fashion for kids. Whatever your fashion vibe – designer label, eco-friendly organic or nostalgia for old-fashioned children's wear – there is plenty of inspiration for your mini me.

The sons of Gwen Stefani and Gavin Rossdale, Kingston and Zuma have inherited their parents' rocker cool, sporting Mohicans and asymmetric hairstyles in the past.

KINGSTON & ZUMA ROSSDALE

It's full-on designer for the youngest of the Beckham clan, who's been wearing Burberry, Stella McCartney, Chloé and Roksanda Ilincic since she was born. But will she be wearing Victoria's high-street Target range or wait for Mum to launch mini-me designer fashion?

Suri, daughter of Katie Holmes and Tom Cruise, has had her three-million-dollar wardrobe closely scrutinised since birth, especially her controversial use of make-up and high heels, including Louboutins, at a young age. But since her parents' divorce her wardrobe has been a lot less designer.

Third in line to the throne, Prince George is much emulated for his classic British style, with mum Catherine choosing old-fashioned corduroy knickerbockers, shorts and dungarees, and nautically themed outfits for her son.

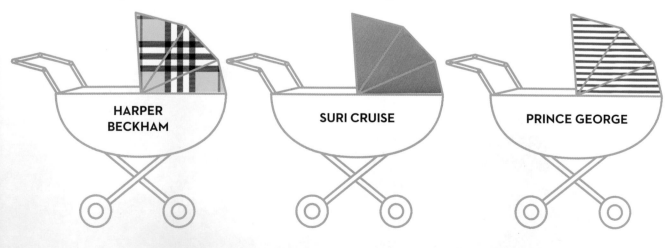

HARPER BECKHAM

SURI CRUISE

PRINCE GEORGE

Son of stylist Rachel Zoe, who has admitted to spending as much time curating her son's wardrobe as her own, Skyler has an edgy vibe with plenty of denim and always his trademark hat.

Jessica Alba says she won't buy designer for daughter Honor and her younger sister, Haven, preferring family hand-me-downs and vintage pieces, which, if anything, make the girls even more stylish.

The twin daughters of *Sex and the City* star Sarah Jessica Parker are predictably well-dressed, though not in Manolos yet, preferring a more colourful, down-to-earth style.

Beyoncé and Jay-Z's daughter thinks nothing of wearing a $2,000 Gucci dress under her denim jacket. The Mischka Aoki dress she wore to accompany her mum to the MTV Video Music Awards reportedly cost $11,000 (and that doesn't include the tiara).

Debuting on the cover of Italian *Teen Vogue* in 2016 alongside her mother, it's no surprise Lila Grace has inherited mum Kate Moss's street-cool fashion sense.

Very much in tune with mum Kim's style vibe, North West wears slip dresses, fur coats and UGGs, dad Kanye's Yeezy brand trainers and sweats, and carries a Louis Vuitton bag. In February 2017 the couple announced they would be launching a kids' clothing line.

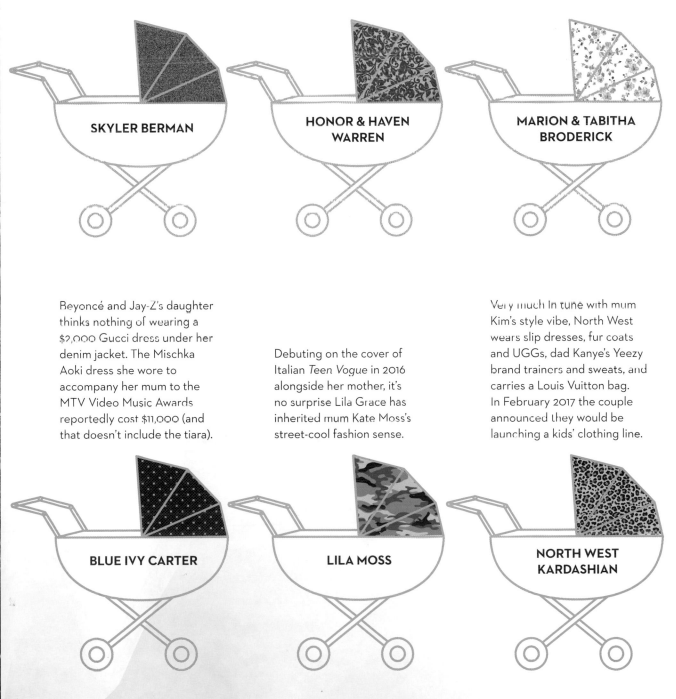

SKYLER BERMAN

HONOR & HAVEN WARREN

MARION & TABITHA BRODERICK

BLUE IVY CARTER

LILA MOSS

NORTH WEST KARDASHIAN

CHAPTER 3

THE FASHION INDUSTRY

The fashion industry is a global juggernaut, from the glamour of the front row at catwalk shows and bespoke haute couture dresses to the way in which high-street retailers quickly translate those seasonal designs and get them in store for fashion lovers around the world. This chapter takes an inside look at the workings of the industry and influences as wide-ranging as pop culture, fashion magazines and advertising, along with major players including legendary fashion editors, supermodels, fashion muses and photographers.

It also questions recent changes to the way we shop and view fashion, including online style and shopping sites, as well as the rise of fashion bloggers and how they have changed the landscape of the fashion industry.

THE FASHION YEAR

In the age of fast fashion and live-streaming of fashion shows, it is not unusual to see a piece from a catwalk show copied and in high-street shops two weeks later. A problem for designers is that they show outfits according to seasons up to six months before the couture pieces hit the stores, meaning that the copycat version is often out there long before the real one. We are also now a global time-zone and season-hopping society, with clothes not always easily categorised into spring/summer and autumn/winter. More versatile are the 'pre-fall' and increasingly important 'resort' collections; the latter was once targeted at wealthy winter sun-seekers, but is now a way for shops to keep less season-specific clothes on the shelves longer than the main collections. With all this in mind, will we soon see the end of the traditional fashion seasons?

THE FASHION YEAR

NOVEMBER/DECEMBER
Resort collections arrive, traditionally featuring bikinis and kaftans and now with more mid-weight everyday clothes with enough longevity to last through a couple of seasons.

JANUARY
Paris Autumn/Winter Haute Couture Fashion Week precedes the main shows. The made-to-measure dresses take four to five months to create for a customer.

FEBRUARY
Spring/summer main collections hit the shops. Autumn/winter fashion weeks give a preview of what will be available the following September.

SEPTEMBER
Spring/summer catwalk shows for the following year are the main event, while autumn/winter ranges arrive in store. Pre-fall is still going strong, bridging the seasons.

MARCH/APRIL
Spring/summer collections are in full swing. Pre-collections are shown to press outside of the show schedule at exclusive locations or in designers' showrooms.

AUGUST
Typically fashion's deadest month; the sales are mostly over, no one can think of autumn yet, but the racks are still stocked with generic pieces from the pre-fall collections.

JULY
Spring/Summer Paris Haute Couture Fashion Week seems timely in July, but this collection is aimed at the following year.

MAY/JUNE
Pre-fall collections begin to hit the stores, giving a lighter taste of the new season. Spring/summer main lines will be on sale towards the middle of June.

PARIS

4 Paris is the finale to the biannual 'big four' fashion weeks. Haute couture has been shown seasonally since 1945 and ready-to-wear (prêt-à-porter) since 1973, both with their own set of shows.

2 The second of the 'big four', launched in 1984. London was the first to coin the term 'fashion week'.

LONDON

MILAN

3 The third of the 'big four', Milan was organised into seasonal groups of shows in 1958.

5 'Curve' plus size fashion festival, Manchester, UK

Mercedes-Benz Fashion Weeks:
  6 Russia
  7 Berlin
  8 Mexico
  9 Istanbul
  10 Australia
  11 China
  12 Amsterdam
  13 Tbilisi, Georgia
  14 Dutch Sustainable Fashion Week
  15 Africa Fashion Week, Nigeria
  16 Swahili Fashion Week, Tanzania
  17 Dakar Fashion Week, Senegal

18 Hub of Africa, Addis Fashion Week, Addis Ababa
19 Fashion Week, Tunis
20 Arab Fashion Week, Dubai
21 Buenos Aires Fashion Week
22 Singapore Fashion Week
23 Stockholm Fashion Week
24 LA Fashion Week
25 MQ Vienna Fashion Week
26 Fiji Fashion Week
27 Belarus Fashion Week
28 Brazil Fashion Week
29 Vancouver Fashion Week
30 Black Fashion Week, Montreal
31 Hong Kong Fashion Week

1 New York is the first of the 'big four' fashion weeks. Design houses have been showing seasonally since 1943.

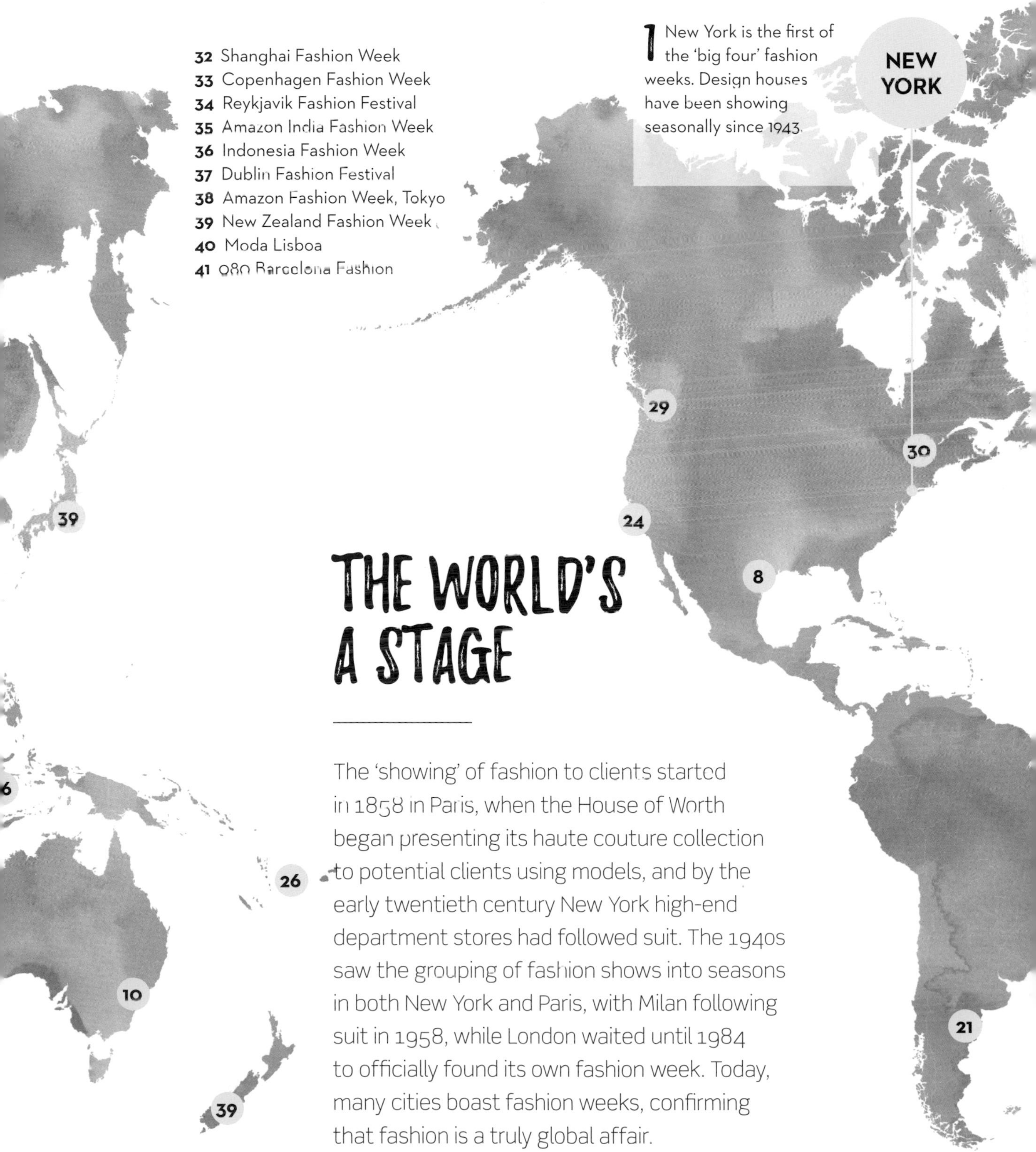

NEW YORK

29

30

39

24

8

THE WORLD'S A STAGE

The 'showing' of fashion to clients started in 1858 in Paris, when the House of Worth began presenting its haute couture collection to potential clients using models, and by the early twentieth century New York high-end department stores had followed suit. The 1940s saw the grouping of fashion shows into seasons in both New York and Paris, with Milan following suit in 1958, while London waited until 1984 to officially found its own fashion week. Today, many cities boast fashion weeks, confirming that fashion is a truly global affair.

6

26

10

21

39

Janice Dickinson claimed to have coined the term 'supermodel' in 1979, but American fashion journalist Judith Cass had in fact used the headline 'Super models are used for fashion shows' back in 1942, and it was also applied to Twiggy in the 1960s. The true era of the supermodel was, however, the late 1980s and 1990s, when a certain model's reputation for not getting out of bed for less than $10,000 a day captured the imagination of millions. For the cover of its January 1990 issue, British *Vogue* commissioned Peter Lindbergh to photograph five supermodels – Cindy Crawford, Naomi Campbell, Linda Evangelista, Christy Turlington and Tatjana Patitz – starting the era of the 'super supers'.

EVOLUTION OF THE SUPERMODEL

1930s–1950s

1950s

The first supermodel was arguably Swedish-born Lisa Fonssagrives, a trained dancer who graced more than 200 covers of *Vogue* in the 1930s, 1940s and 1950s , working with photographers including George Hoyningen-Huene, Man Ray, Horst, George Platt Lynes, Irving Penn (whom she married) and Richard Avedon.

US-born aristocrat Dovima was the highest paid model of the 1950s, famously posing with elephants for Richard Avedon and *Harper's Bazaar* in 1955. Meanwhile Suzy Parker, the face of Revlon cosmetics, was the first model to earn over $100,000 a year, inspiring Audrey Hepburn's character in the 1957 film *Funny Face*.

1960s

1970s

1980s–1990s

2000s

The first of the new breed of super-slim models was Jean Shrimpton, aka 'The Shrimp', though Twiggy is the best-known super-skinny 1960s model. Meanwhile, Veruschka, the daughter of a Russian count, was the first model to become known by her first name alone.

The 1970s spawned several iconic models, including leggy Texan blonde Jerry Hall, discovered sunbathing on a beach in St Tropez; Japanese-American Marie Helvin, famous for doing her last lingerie shoot at the age of sixty-two; the all-American Cheryl Tiegs; Playboy-bunny-turned-model Lauren Hutton, and statuesque Somalian model Iman, the first black supermodel.

The era of the Big Five: Cindy Crawford, Naomi Campbell, Linda Evangelista, Christy Turlington and Tatjana Patitz. The first four opened Versace's 1991 couture show, a defining moment of the supermodel. Other big names from this era include Elle 'The Body' Macpherson; Claudia Schiffer and Kate Moss, whose more edgy waif-like look marked a new age of the supermodel.

Since 2000 the cult of the supermodel has died down, with arguably only Gisele Bündchen claiming such a status, although Natalia Vodianova and Cara Delevingne have come close. Today we are seeing the rise of models such as Gigi Hadid and Kendall Jenner who have risen to the top of the industry through hard work and the allure of their millions of social media followers.

A LIFE IN STYLE
KATE MOSS

She is the ultimate cool girl and off-beat style icon, yet Kate Moss's arrival on the fashion scene was an unlikely one. Not quite tall enough at 5ft 7in and waif-skinny at a time when supermodels were of Cindy Crawford's athletic-curves build, fifteen-year-old Moss's first big shoot was for *The Face* magazine in 1990. Shot by Corinne Day on Camber Sands in Kent, the model was captured smoking a cigarette and posing topless; the images' raw, immediate feel was the antithesis of the glossy fashion shoots of the time. Shortly afterwards she was booked as the face of Calvin Klein and the rest, as they say, is history.

FREE SPIRIT
Kate is a lover of all thing boho, wearing big printed dresses, gypsy tunics and even going barefoot at times. As in all things however, she is stylish enough to mix it up and unafraid to pair floaty floral prints with spike-heeled black leather boots. A rock groupie and party girl at heart, Kate is perfectly at home in the mud of a music festival wearing tiny shorts and wellington boots.

DESIGN FOR THE HIGH STREET
In the past, Kate was never a high-street shopper, even as a teenager preferring vintage finds when she couldn't afford designer, but that changed in 2008 thanks to her sought-after collections for Topshop, where she took her years of experience of the cut and styling of designer labels to create affordable fashion for us all. The model has also appeared as the face of many high-street brands, most recently appearing in a high-profile campaign for Poland's answer to Topshop, the fashion store Reserved.

1 GLAM ROCK
Kate Moss is a long-time fan of furry, hairy jackets and coats worn over anything from skinny ripped jeans to glamorous full-length evening gowns. The allure of a gold dress is a favourite for evening wear, often vintage or designed by her close friend Marc Jacobs.

2 VINTAGE
Kate has always loved vintage fashion, such as this lemon-yellow dress she bought from LA vintage store Lily et Cie and wore to a party in 2003. This dress was the inspiration behind one of the most popular items from the model's 2014 Topshop collection.

3 BLAZER AND SKINNY JEANS
Kate has perfected chic everyday style in a blazer and rolled-up skinny jeans, often over a statement t-shirt and always accessorised with sunglasses.

A BEAUTIFUL WORLD

Fashion still struggles with diversity and is often criticised for the narrow definition of beauty it projects. The nations producing the most models overall today are the expected heavyweights - United States, Brazil, Russia, UK and the Netherlands – although this shifts slightly when we look at the number of models per capita. Fortunately, a growing numbers of models from around the world are hitting fashion heights and runways, and advertising campaigns are becoming increasingly ethnically diverse as a consequence.

Nations producing the most models

1. United States
2. Brazil
3. Russia
4. United Kingdom
5. Netherlands
6. Canada
7. Germany
8. Poland
9. Australia
10. France

Top ten model-producing nations per capita

1. Estonia
2. Iceland
3. Lithuania
4. Denmark
5. Latvia
6. Sweden
7. Netherlands
8. Slovakia
9. Norway
10. Czech Republic

NORTH AMERICA
Canada: Linda Evangelista
United States: Gigi and Bella Hadid, Cindy Crawford, Jerry Hall, Kendall Jenner, Karlie Kloss, Kate Upton, Ashley Graham, Natalie Westling

SOUTH AMERICA
Argentina: Mica Agarñaraz
Brazil: Gisele Bündchen, Adriana Lima, Alessandra Ambrosio, Lais Ribeiro

EUROPE

Denmark: Helena Christensen
Estonia: Carmen Kass, Karmen Pedaru, Elisabeth Erm
France: Inès de la Fressange, Laetitia Casta, Constance Jablonski
Germany: Claudia Schiffer, Tatjana Patitz, Heidi Klum
Italy: Carla Bruni, Benedetta Barzini, Isabella Rossellini, Vittoria Ceretti
Latvia: Ginta Lapiņa
Lithuania: Edita Vilkevičiūtė, Svetlana Lazareva
Martinique: Karly Loyce

Netherlands: Doutzen Kroes, Lara Stone, Karen Mulder, Kiki Willems, Imaan Hammam, Rianne van Rompaey
Russia: Natalia Vodianova, Irina Shayk, Valery Kaufman
Slovakia: Linda Nývltová, Michaela Kocianova
Spain: Eugenia Silva, Clara Alonso
Sweden: Elin Nordegren, Elsa Hosk
Ukraine: Milla Jovovich, Daria Werbowy
United Kingdom: Kate Moss, Naomi Campbell, Cara Delevingne, Rosie Huntington-Whiteley, Jourdan Dunn, Twiggy, Karen Elson, Neelam Gill, Ruth Bell

ASIA

China: Liu Wen, Jing Wen
India: Bhumika Arora, Pooja Mor
Israel: Bar Refaeli

AFRICA

Angola: Maria Borges
Somalia: Iman
South Africa: Candice Swanepoel
South Sudan: Alek Wek

AUSTRALASIA

Australia: Elle Macpherson, Miranda Kerr
New Zealand: Kylie Bax, Stella Maxwell

FASHION FRONT ROW

Fashion shows are as much about being seen as viewing the new collections. It is the job of a designer's publicist to decide who is worthy of a front row seat – a balancing act between top fashion editors, celebrities and important fashion buyers.

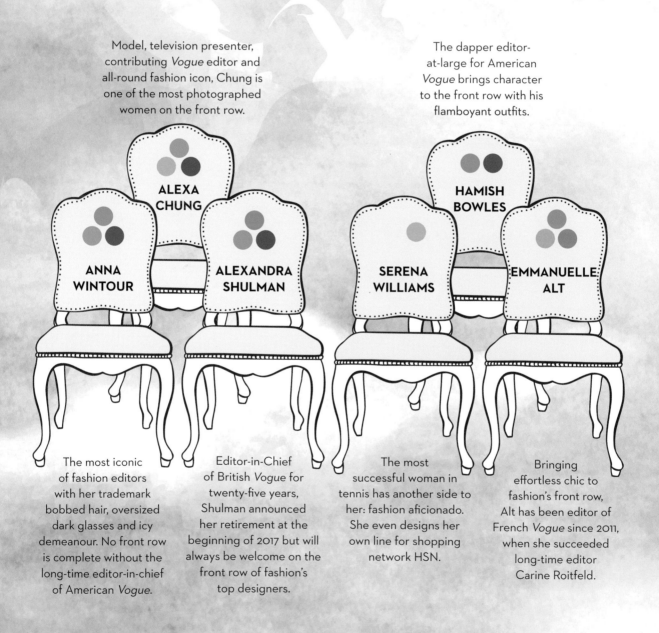

Model, television presenter, contributing *Vogue* editor and all-round fashion icon, Chung is one of the most photographed women on the front row.

The dapper editor-at-large for American *Vogue* brings character to the front row with his flamboyant outfits.

ALEXA CHUNG

HAMISH BOWLES

ANNA WINTOUR

ALEXANDRA SHULMAN

SERENA WILLIAMS

EMMANUELLE ALT

The most iconic of fashion editors with her trademark bobbed hair, oversized dark glasses and icy demeanour. No front row is complete without the long-time editor-in-chief of American *Vogue*.

Editor-in-Chief of British *Vogue* for twenty-five years, Shulman announced her retirement at the beginning of 2017 but will always be welcome on the front row of fashion's top designers.

The most successful woman in tennis has another side to her: fashion aficionado. She even designs her own line for shopping network HSN.

Bringing effortless chic to fashion's front row, Alt has been editor of French *Vogue* since 2011, when she succeeded long-time editor Carine Roitfeld.

GRAPHIC KEY:

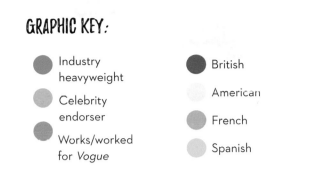

- Industry heavyweight
- Celebrity endorser
- Works/worked for *Vogue*

- British
- American
- French
- Spanish

Socialite and sometime actress Olivia Palermo is regularly photographed at fashion shows across the world, never failing to produce a new outfit.

Actress, model and fashion designer, Sienna Miller is another front row stalwart regularly gracing the shows' prime real estate.

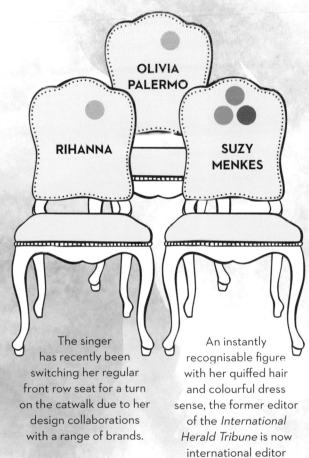

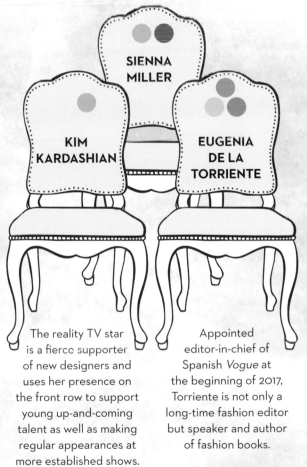

OLIVIA PALERMO

RIHANNA

SUZY MENKES

SIENNA MILLER

KIM KARDASHIAN

EUGENIA DE LA TORRIENTE

The singer has recently been switching her regular front row seat for a turn on the catwalk due to her design collaborations with a range of brands.

An instantly recognisable figure with her quiffed hair and colourful dress sense, the former editor of the *International Herald Tribune* is now international editor for all nineteen editions of *Vogue* online.

The reality TV star is a fierce supporter of new designers and uses her presence on the front row to support young up-and-coming talent as well as making regular appearances at more established shows.

Appointed editor-in-chief of Spanish *Vogue* at the beginning of 2017, Torriente is not only a long-time fashion editor but speaker and author of fashion books.

THE LINE OF BEAUTY

Catwalk shows do not just showcase the latest fashion: beauty trends start there too, and the make-up artist is an essential part of the success of a show. Celebrity make-up artists such as Pat McGrath, Charlotte Tilbury and Tom Pecheux command huge fees and have their own make-up ranges, but there are also many jobbing make-up artists who form the teams for make-up brands and follow the lead artist's design. At London Fashion Week's spring/summer shows in 2016, MAC Cosmetics had 484 make-up artists backstage and spent more than 12,000 hours between them attending to more than 5,200 models.

1. PRE-SHOW PREPARATION

A make-up artist will talk to a fashion designer a couple of months before fashion week to get an idea of the look of the collection and any themes featured in the show. If the designer has some particular influences for that season, the make-up artist will then do additional research before they meet.

4. SHOW DAY SET UP

Pressure is high on show day, with up to forty models per show and a team of make-up artists under the direction of a senior make-up artist. Make-up artists arrive as early as five o'clock in the morning to set up their station, and will then have a last-minute debrief with the designer or his PR to confirm the number of models and amount of time allocated to each one.

2. MAKE-UP TEST

A few days, or even the day before the show, the make-up artist will meet with the designer and stylist to look at fabric swatches or actual pieces for the show, along with any inspiration and beauty references. Between them they will test a variety of looks on a model.

3. MAKE-UP KIT

A make-up artist's full kit is immense, so most will narrow it down for the shows, packing concise kits for individual shows. Packing a make-up case so that powders do not turn to dust and foundations do not leak is an art form in itself.

5. PRE-SHOW PRESSURE

The first thing a make-up artist does when the rest of the team arrives is demo the look on a model; being able to oversee a make-up team efficiently is essential. There is little time to correct errors, as artists sometimes have as little as three and never more than thirty minutes to complete the look. Top supermodels sometimes arrive just five minutes before their catwalk appearance.

6. A DAY BACKSTAGE

Alongside making-up big-name models and checking on the work of their team, make-up artists dodge photographers trying to capture the look of the model they are working on and are interviewed by beauty journalists and bloggers. Staying calm in the face of designers altering the look last-minute, junior artists making mistakes and models arriving late is all part of the job.

TOUJOURS COUTURE

Haute couture outfits are often described as having no price tag. The huge amount of time, money and skill needed to create a bespoke garment means that these one-off creations can cost tens – or even hundreds – of thousands of pounds.

Haute couture translates literally as 'high dressmaking', and those lucky enough to commission such garments are rewarded by exquisite items that show a level of artistry unattainable elsewhere in the fashion industry. For a fashion house to qualify as haute couture they must meet the standards laid down by the Chambre Syndicale de la Haute Couture and the Chambre de Commerce et d'Industrie in Paris, following a particular set of rules concerning, for example, number of fittings for each client and the number of technical staff employed to make the clothes. Haute couture houses must present two collections of fifty unique garments each year, in January and July.

An invitation to an haute couture show is not easy to get. Clients need a personal introduction from a stylist or another client, and are carefully vetted for their suitability and financial means. A client who wears a couture outfit is a representative of the brand and therefore needs to behave accordingly!

If you see a piece you like, the next step is to make an appointment in the salon to discuss your unique version of the garment. Up to five fittings will be needed requiring as many as 150 measurements. Couture houses make, and keep, life-size measurement-exact mannequins of their loyal clients.

A pair of trousers or a day dress can cost £10,000 ($13,000) or more, but elaborate evening wear can cost upwards of £150,000 ($200,000).

Given the expense of these outfits, many are created for high-profile occasions such as the Oscars. In 2016, the twenty nominees for best actor and actress wore an astonishing £570,000 ($749,252) worth of couture.

Surprisingly, given these price tags, most haute couture makes a loss. But, from a marketing point of view, the chance to showcase the superb skill and craftsmanship of the world's best designers and dressmakers is priceless.

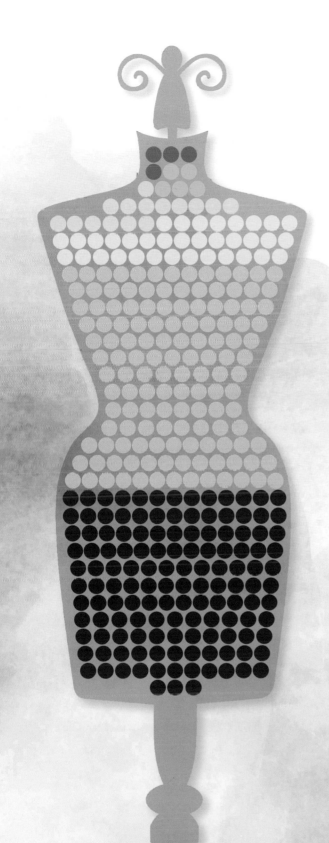

HAUTE COUTURE BY NUMBERS

4
months to fit an outfit

5
fittings required for each client

20
seamstresses at least to be employed by the atelier

35
outfits required for an haute couture show

150
hours needed to attach 50,000 Swarovski crystals to a single dress

150
measurements taken to ensure the garment is the correct size

CATWALK TO HIGH STREET

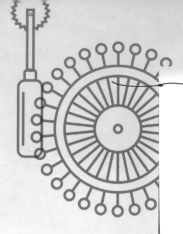

Before fashion shows were live-streamed on the internet with photos appearing on social media as the models strut down the catwalk, high-street retailers, typically forbidden from attending shows, had to work hard to get images of the designs so that they could copy them for the mass market. Today, fast fashion sees copies of designs hit the stores mere weeks later.

MANUFACTURE

Sourcing or printing fabric and manufacture typically takes eight to ten weeks, but high-street store Zara's model of having in-house designers and a manufacturing team within Europe means clothes can be produced in just two to four weeks. Fast-fashion retailers think nothing of stocking new, on-trend items every week. Ironically, a designer version might not hit the stores for six months after being showcased on the catwalk.

DESIGNER CATWALK SHOW

Images of distinctive designs are often readily available, although some designers, such as Tom Ford, have held 'closed' shows to avoid copycat designs. Some retailers have pattern cutters on standby to instantly copy an iconic look. They will also look at overall fashions for colour and shape, and will consider many designers to highlight the next big trends.

SIMPLIFYING THE DESIGN

For the high street, designs are significantly simpler and cannot be a direct copy. Shapes will be tweaked, colourways subtly changed and detailing altered. The cost of being sued by a designer for copying a design is huge – in 2007 Topshop had to pay £12,000 compensation after Chloé brought legal action over a yellow minidress.

SALES

Zara also pioneered a production model that is now widely copied, of producing smaller quantities of a greater number of designs. Not only does this make the item covetable, it also solves the problem of surplus stock. The fast turnaround makes this possible. If demand is high, more can be produced; if not, a new design can replace the old one quickly.

PREVENTING COPYCAT DESIGNS

Copyright in fashion is notoriously hard to enforce, but design patents are a solution for some items, such as shoes. Nike and Adidas have patents on all their designs. Some designer handbags have patents, as do recognisable style details. While patents are costly and time-consuming, trademarks can be a better bet as logos can't be reproduced.

COST

The big draw for fashion lovers is the price of copycat fashions, which at most cost tens of pounds instead of thousands for the designer piece. The Topshop version of the Chloé dress it had to withdraw cost £35 versus £185, and in 2006 Marks & Spencer similarly got rid of a silk jewel-buckled evening bag costing £9.50 that Jimmy Choo claimed was a direct copy of its £495 Cosmo bag.

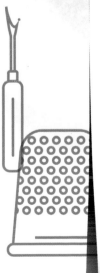
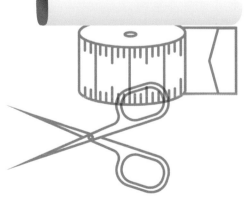

THE GREAT BEAUTIES

GRAPHIC KEY

muse
other relationship
combination

Few industries are as interconnected as the fashion world. The ultimate accolade, of course, is to become a fashion muse – the source of creative inspiration to a designer and the embodiment of their style.

KARL LAGERFELD has been inspired by many stylish women including Diane Kruger and Kim Kardashian.

INES DE LA FRESSANGE was a muse to Lagerfeld in the 1980s before a dramatic fallout.

LADY AMANDA HARLECH met Galliano in 1984 and became his 'more than a muse'. She similarly inspired Karl Lagerfeld.

JOHN GALLIANO headed Givenchy from 1995 to 1996 before leaving for Dior.

KATE MOSS chose Galliano to design her wedding dress in 2011. She is best friends with Naomi Campbell.

MARC JACOBS counts muse Kate Moss as a close friend, along with Naomi Campbell.

NAOMI CAMPBELL reunited with fellow 1990s supers for the 2017 Versace show in Milan.

GRACE JONES was dressed by the Tunisian designer for the 1985 Bond film *A View to a Kill*.

AZZEDINE ALAÏA was inspired by the ferocious energy of Grace Jones, and later Naomi Campbell.

JEAN-PAUL GAULTIER created the iconic cone bra for the Blond Ambition tour in 1990.

DITA VON TEESE launched a lingerie line with her good friend Louboutin.

MADONNA The singer has modelled for Gaultier, and worn Louboutins in her music videos.

CHRISTIAN LOUBOUTIN designs custom high heels for his muse to wear in her burlesque shows.

YVES ST LAURENT In 2012 the company was taken to court over their use of red-soled shoes.

DONATELLA VERSACE is strikingly similar to her muse and friend, Lady Gaga.

LADY GAGA Famous 'frenemy' of Madonna, the singer has appeared as the face of Versace.

LOULOU DE LA FALAISE felt the title 'muse' did not reflect her hard work for the label.

HUBERT GIVENCHY designed Hepburn's most iconic dresses and was a lifelong friend.

ALEXANDER MCQUEEN The well-connected designer was at Givenchy from 1996 to 2001.

ISABELLA BLOW carried off Treacy's most flamboyant creations, including an entire galleon ship.

AUDREY HEPBURN wore her first Givenchy outfit in the 1954 film *Sabrina*.

ANNABELLE NEILSON The socialite was introduced to McQueen by the stylist Isabella Blow.

PHILIP TREACY was introduced to McQueen by Isabella Blow and the two often collaborated.

BEHIND THE LENS

RICHARD AVEDON

In his long career, Avedon captured the most iconic faces of the twentieth century and transformed fashion photography, replacing beautiful yet expressionless still lifes with portraits that allowed models to show their personalities. The images, filled with expression, vulnerability and playfulness, spoke to the viewer. One of Avedon's most famous shoots was 'Dovima with Elephants', shot in 1955, which depicted the model in full evening dress flanked by circus elephants.

NICK KNIGHT

Nick Knight has brought a bold creativity to fashion photography in his collaborations with designers such as John Galliano and Alexander McQueen. His experiments with cutting-edge technology have led to images filled with light, colour and movement, often with elements designed to shock. In 2000 he launched SHOWstudio.com, a fashion and film website that continues to push artistic boundaries. Knight's high-profile music videos also earn him creative acclaim.

HORST

Horst P. Horst's photographic career spanned an incredible six decades, kicking off in 1931. The American-German photographer is known for his striking portraits, in which he pushed stylistic boundaries to become one of the most iconic photographers of all time. In his collaborations with French, British and American *Vogue*, Horst gave celebrities an untouchable yet alluring quality that has inspired other fashion photographers since.

ANNIE LEIBOVITZ

Best-known for her celebrity portraits and contributions to *Vanity Fair* magazine, Annie Leibovitz has made an important contribution to fashion photography, often using the same theatrical style evident in her portraiture. Her images for *Vogue* are other-worldly, filled with references to childrens' tales and legends, and with a clarity of line and colour that makes them instantly recognisable.

HELMUT NEWTON

Known for provocative and sometimes explicit images that have earned him the nickname the 'king of kink', Helmut Newton is an important contributor to the world of fashion photography. Perhaps his most famous fashion image is his 1975 image of Yves St Laurent's 'Le Smoking' suit.

IRVING PENN

As a contributor to *Vogue* from the 1940s, Irving Penn's images have a painterly quality reminiscent of the Grand Masters. His use of black and white in striking contrast characterises his early work – especially those images featuring his wife, the model Lisa Fonssagrives. But his focus on simplicity and clarity lasted his whole career. Penn famously used few props and simple single-source lighting.

STEVEN MEISEL

Steven Meisel has never been afraid of shooting radical fashion images, often for Italian *Vogue* – in fact, he has shot every one of the magazine's covers since its launch in 1988. Revered by models and celebrities as a true artist, he is known for being bold enough to use images to speak his mind.

MARIO TESTINO

Peruvian-born Mario Testino is arguably the world's most prolific portrait and fashion photographer – he estimates he has shot Kate Moss several thousand times – and his 1997 *Vanity Fair* images of Diana, Princess of Wales, made him a household name. Testino's luxe style, with plenty of colour, glamour and gloss, has made him a favourite of both fashion editors and designers.

DAVID BAILEY

David Bailey's name is synonymous with images of the swinging sixties, when his photographs for *Vogue* helped seal the reputation of Twiggy and Jean Shrimpton. Another favourite muse is Kate Moss, who has been photographed by Bailey numerous times. A pioneer of modern photography, always drawn to portraiture, his memorable images include Mick Jagger, John Lennon and Paul McCartney and a host of characters from his native East End of London.

ENTER THE BLOGOSPHERE

The war between young, self-starting fashion bloggers and fashion editors who feel they have earned their style credentials over decades in the business rages on. At Milan Fashion Week in 2016 American *Vogue* editors, including Sally Singer, accused the fashion bloggers of 'heralding the death of style' as they changed their paid-to-wear outfits every hour, uploading endless shots to their Instagram feeds, all the while fighting to get themselves snapped by the fashion paparazzi. Others disagree, of course, seeing the young stylistas as fashion voices far more influential than the stuck-in-the-mud editors, and their huge followings on social media, collaborations with big-name designers and appearance on fashion magazine covers suggest they might just have a point.

CHIARA FERRAGNI

11.2m Instagram followers
The Italian-born, LA-based model and designer blogs at *The Blonde Salad*.

AIMEE SONG

4.7m Instagram followers
One of the earliest fashion blogs, also showcasing Aimee Song's interior design, *Song of Style* receives two million page views per month.

SHEA MARIE

1.1m Instagram followers
The style guru blogs at *Peace Love Shea*, mixing California-girl sunniness with a boho and rock chic.

Instagram followings correct as of November 2017

HELENA BORDON

1m Instagram followers
The Brazilian blogger has fashion in her blood – her mother is the style director of Brazilian *Vogue* – and Bordon is also joint owner of Brazilian fast-fashion label 284.

BRYANBOY
663k Instagram followers
Filipino Bryan Grey Yambao founded his celebrity fashion and style blog in 2004 and it is recognised as one of the most influential in the field, Marc Jacobs is such a fan he named his BB bag in Yambao's honour. His blog gets over one million hits per month.

TANESHA AWASTHI
289k Instagram followers
The founder of award-wining plus-sized blog *Girl With Curves* offers modern, sophisticated styles with a touch of edginess and proves size should never limit style.

SUSIE BUBBLE
384k Instagram followers
UK style blogger Susie Lau writes *Style Bubble*, reputedly attending 140 shows per season.

ALEX STEDMAN
152k Instagram followers
Former shopping editor for *Red* magazine, the now-freelance stylist offers tips and anecdotes about staying stylish on a budget at *The Frugality*.

PHIL OH
157k Instagram followers
The blogger behind Mr *Street Peeper*, Phil travels the world snapping style on the street and at fashion shows as well as contributing to international fashion magazines.

SARA CRAMPTON
560k Instagram followers
The Australian blogger at *Harper and Harley* focuses on laid-back Aussie style, minimalist chic and fashion essentials.

RITA SARAQI
27.5k Instagram followers
The first fashion blogger to come out of Kosovo blogs at *Fishnets and Rainbows*, has collaborated with Benetton and Mango and is part of a movement among Kosovo's young to rebrand the country after its independence in 2008.

CHARLOTTE GROENEVELD
326k Instagram followers
The Dutch-born, New-York based mother-of-two blogs at *The Fashion Guitar*. She collaborates with designers but makes a point of keeping her style ethos and blog content for real women.

IN VOGUE

Launched by Arthur Baldwin Turnure in 1892 as a weekly magazine in the United States, *Vogue* as we know it today took off when upmarket publisher Condé Nast bought the magazine in 1905. American *Vogue* was the only edition until 1916 when the British edition was launched, and the fashion bible has never looked back, now boasting twenty-one international editions.

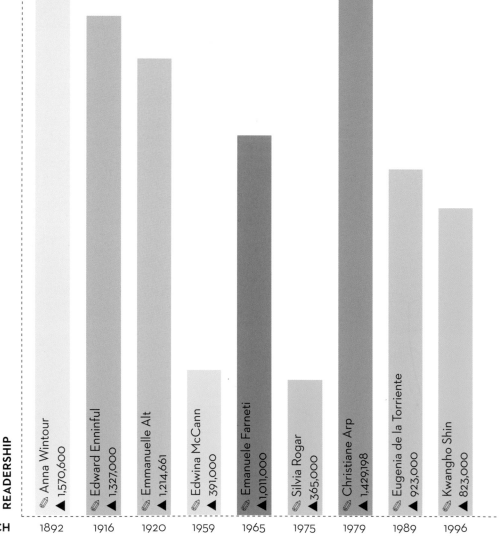

READERSHIP

Anna Wintour ▲ 1,570,600

Edward Enninful ▲ 1,327,000

Emmanuelle Alt ▲ 1,214,661

Edwina McCann ▲ 391,000

Emanuele Farneti ▲ 1,011,000

Silvia Rogar ▲ 365,000

Christiane Arp ▲ 1,429,198

Eugenia de la Torriente ▲ 923,000

Kwangho Shin ▲ 823,000

DATE OF LAUNCH   1892   1916   1920   1959   1965   1975   1979   1989   1996

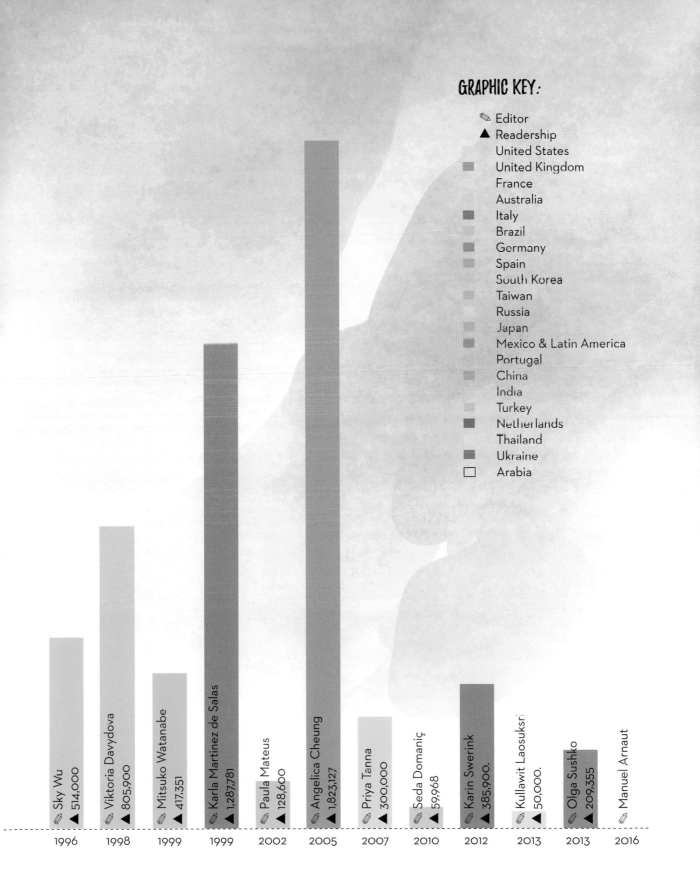

✏ Editor
▲ Readership
  United States
  United Kingdom
  France
  Australia
  Italy
  Brazil
  Germany
  Spain
  South Korea
  Taiwan
  Russia
  Japan
  Mexico & Latin America
  Portugal
  China
  India
  Turkey
  Netherlands
  Thailand
  Ukraine
□ Arabia

✏ Sky Wu ▲ 514,000 — 1996
✏ Viktoria Davydova ▲ 805,900 — 1998
✏ Mitsuko Watanabe ▲ 417,351 — 1999
✏ Karla Martinez de Salas ▲ 1,287,781 — 1999
✏ Paula Mateus ▲ 128,600 — 2002
✏ Angelica Cheung ▲ 1,823,127 — 2005
✏ Priya Tanna ▲ 300,000 — 2007
✏ Seda Domaniç ▲ 59,968 — 2010
✏ Karin Swerink ▲ 385,900. — 2012
✏ Kullawit Laosuksri ▲ 50,000. — 2013
✏ Olga Sushko ▲ 209,355 — 2013
✏ Manuel Arnaut — 2016

THE DEVIL WEARS...

Fashion editors are some of the most powerful players in the industry, able to launch an unknown designer or model, effect controversial change through editorial choices and shape the way fashion evolves.

DIANA VREELAND

Born in Paris but raised in New York, Diana Vreeland is the doyenne of fashion editors. She kicked off her career at *Harper's Bazaar* in 1936, where she stirred up the tame clothes of the day, famously stating that 'too much good taste can be boring'. After more than twenty years of outlandish fashion, Vreeland moved to *Vogue* in 1963, where her over-the-top fashion spreads were legendary. Unfortunately, the costs of these shoots were equally extravagant and Vreeland was fired in 1971, but she is still revered by many as the world's most important contributor to fashion editorial.

GRACE CODDINGTON

Born on the small Welsh island of Anglesey in 1941, as a child Grace Coddington dreamed of being part of the fashion world. A successful model in the 1960s, after a car accident Coddington moved into fashion editorial, joining British *Vogue* in 1968 and American *Vogue* twenty years later. There, she employed a deeply creative approach to fashion styling and photography. Though she left *Vogue* in 2016, her striking red mane still appears at fashion shows and events.

FRANCA SOZZANI

Editor of Italian *Vogue* from 1988 until her death in 2016, Sozzani was unafraid to break fashion taboos. Her achievements included an all-black issue in 2008, and a twenty-page spread of plus-size models in 2011. She also drew attention to ethical issues beyond the fashion world: her Gulf of Mexico oil spill spread, shot by Steven Meisel, featured Kristen McMenamy in the poses of oil-drenched animals. Sozzani is credited with launching the supermodel phenomenon, by putting the models' names alongside their images in the 1990s.

SUZY MENKES

Born in Britain in 1943, Suzy Menkes is an unmistakable figure on the fashion circuit, with her trademark rolled quiff. But she is most admired for her fierce but fair writing style, which accurately assesses trends whilst also placing fashion in a wider context. Menkes worked for the *International Herald Tribune* for twenty-six years and in 2014 became Condé Nast's international editor, overseeing all international issues of *Vogue*.

ANNA WINTOUR

An iconic presence, with her immaculate bob and dark glasses, Anna Wintour became fashion editor of *Harper's Bazaar* in New York in her twenties, before moving though *Viva*, *Savvy* and *New York* magazines to become editor of British *Vogue*. She was lured back to the United States as editor-in-chief in 1988, where she has remained ever since. Nicknamed 'Nuclear Wintour' for her icy style, she has nevertheless become an indomitable force in the fashion industry.

CARINE ROITFELD

French-Russian Carine Roitfeld edited French *Vogue* for ten years from 2001, in which time she broke many taboos, taking advantage of liberal French attitudes to shoot avant-garde fashion features, including a 2007 cover featuring thirteen models tied up with a curtain rod. Often on the most-stylish-women-in-the-world lists, Roitfeld has since designed for Uniqlo, launched her own magazine, *CR Fashion Book*, and also works as the global fashion director of *Harper's Bazaar*.

ALEXANDRA SHULMAN

The former editor-in-chief of British *Vogue*, who left the magazine in 2017, after exactly twenty-five years and one day, she's often cited as the opposite to Anna Wintour, both in personal and editorial style. Instead of overly glossy and expensive fashion shoots, Shulman developed a reputation for more creative and original features. She found the idea that she didn't 'look' like the editor of *Vogue* ridiculous, rightly stating, 'I am the editor of *Vogue*...so what else does the editor of *Vogue* look like?'

EDWARD ENNINFUL

The high-profile, Instagram-loving fashion editor was a surprise appointment to succeed Alexandra Shulman at British *Vogue* in 2017, resulting in a big shake-up of the magazine's editorial team and a new influx of celebrity contributing editors, including his best friend Naomi Campbell. Ghanaian-born Enninful is tipped to bring a new, edgy feel to *Vogue*, not surprising from the man who edited *i-D* magazine at just eighteen and who notoriously pushes fashion boundaries: he put together the all-black issue of Italian *Vogue* in 2008.

STORY TIME

While the aim of a fashion shoot is in part to showcase the latest designs and give editorial coverage to big advertisers, it is also a chance to create a work of art, especially if a big-name photographer and models are involved. This is how a fashion magazine creates a fashion spread.

STORY BOARD

Putting together a story board prior to the shoot itself helps to make sure the images tell a 'story'.

CASTING & LOCATION

Finding the right model for the job is essential for creating the desired look. If the shoot is going to be featured on the cover, the model needs to be a face that sells magazines. Shoots are often in studios but many are on location, meaning that flights and hotels will need to be booked for models, the editorial team, photographers, hair and make-up artists and stylists. The art department is responsible for sourcing any props.

EDITORIAL BRIEFING

Editor, stylist and art director meet with the photographer to outline the brief and budget for the fashion story. Ideas for models, locations and clothes are discussed and tear sheets, mood boards and digital imagery help form a cohesive theme for the shoot. The number of pages are allocated for the feature.

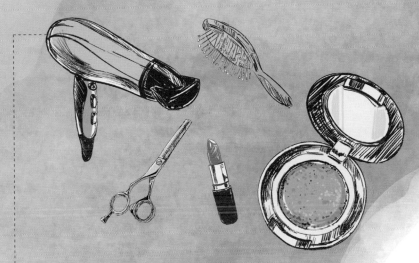

STYLING, HAIR & MAKE-UP

The skill of a good stylist is essential to find the right clothes to create the mood of the shoot. Showcasing the latest fashion trends, mixing top-end designer pieces with high-street fashion, choosing accessories and finding new and interesting ways to put together outfits are all part of the job. Sample clothes are called in from fashion PR firms or designers, with options in case the original outfits don't work. Hair and make-up designers can quickly interpret the look the stylists are after.

THE SHOOT

Good photographers will create an atmosphere to get the right mood for the shoot, usually with the aim of relaxing the models, but sometimes challenging them to create something surprising. The photographer and their assistants are responsible for lighting, most using the latest in digital technology and taking thousands of photographs to select from. Days are long and tiring. The fashion team takes Polaroids to make sure they know exactly which clothes and accessories are used. A multi-page fashion spread is usually shot over several days.

POST-PRODUCTION

Images are chosen and touched up ready for publication, with blemishes and imperfections removed.

FINISHING TOUCH

The debate over digitally altering images is a heated one, with a lack of consensus over the impact these images have on body image. Fashion magazines still digitally retouch all their photos, sometimes only removing minor blemishes, but often significantly altering them to create an entirely unobtainable image. The selfie generation also use filters and apps to present a glamorised image of themselves to the world. Some argue that we want these aspirational images of models and celebrities, and view images knowing they are retouched; others campaign fiercely for Photoshopped images to be banned. So what do you think?

Some high-profile cosmetic brands have been censored for digitally enhancing images. A 2012 Rimmel ad was banned for using lash inserts on Georgia May Jagger. A year earlier, CoverGirl also had an ad banned for enhancing Taylor Swift's lashes in post-production.

In 2014, singer Lorde posted pictures of her acne to show the reality of her skin.

Keira Knightley objected to digital enhancement of her breasts on publicity posters for the film *King Arthur* in 2004 and subsequently posed topless for *Interview* magazine in 2014 to show her real physique.

Kate Winslet, who publicly complained about *GQ* magazine reducing the size of her legs by around a third in a 2003 edition, produced a Polaroid of the real image saying she thought she 'looked pretty good' in it.

40% of American women stated they would consider cosmetic surgery.

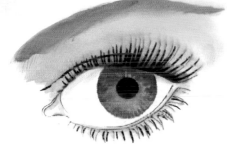

80% of women in the United States say images of women in the media make them feel insecure.

81% of ten-year-olds in the United States are afraid of being fat.

90% of fifteen- to seventeen-year-old American girls want to change at least one aspect of their physical appearance.

LET'S DANCE

Pop culture has long influenced fashion and the intersection between the music and fashion industries seems increasingly significant. Today we are seeing creative collaborations between pop stars and major designers, and haute couture in music videos and concerts worn by global stars such as Beyoncé and Lady Gaga.

SEX PISTOLS

As part of the punk rock scene, the anarchist group the Sex Pistols, with their love of ripped, torn and dirty second-hand clothing and t-shirts with slogans most people would baulk at displaying, should have been the antithesis of fashion. Nevertheless, thanks to Vivienne Westwood (see page 117), punk fashion took off and has remained influential ever since, with designers such as Versace using the safety pin in many designs, and the trend for ripped, distressed and deconstructed clothes enduring to this day.

BOB MARLEY

Bob Marley's relaxed look and laid-back attitude made him one of the greatest stars of music, and also started a trend for wearing military surplus, especially his trademark M-65 jacket. His Rastafari colours also had an enduring fashion influence, with both streetwear and designer fashion appearing in the ubiquitous stripes. Marley's love of Adidas trainers and track-suit bottoms pre-dated the hip-hop revolution and started making this casual sportswear fashionable.

MADONNA

The queen of reinvention, Madge has given us many different looks, some more dubious than others (Jean Paul Gaultier braless corset anyone?). But her most influential style period was the 1980s and her *Desperately Seeking Susan* look: dirty white lace tights and fingerless gloves, hair bows and bandeau-style head wraps, studded boots, religious necklaces and large hoop earrings. The look was copied by every teenage girl and is one that still influences fashion today.

KURT COBAIN

In the 1990s the Nirvana frontman popularised the grunge look. Messy and unkempt, grunge focused on ripped jeans, flannel shirts and lumberjack workwear. Cobain's wife Courtney Love popularised a spin-off style, the 'kinderwhore' look, with babydoll or cute floral dresses paired with ripped tights, boots or Mary Janes, smudged, heavy make-up and messed-up hair (see page 124).

MICHAEL JACKSON

The troubled star had a unique fashion aesthetic that included studded, military-style, varsity letter and moto jackets; tight red leather trousers; sharp-cut suits; hats and sunglasses. His influence was wide-reaching and his much-copied *Thriller* jacket eventually sold in 2011 for $1.8 million (£1.4 million).

KANYE WEST

The maverick wrapper and lover of designer brands, most famously popularising Paris's Vetements, is considered by many to be the man who brought high fashion and hip hop together. He has collaborated with Nike, Louis Vuitton and now Adidas on sneaker lines and with A.P.C. on a menswear collection. His signature look is relaxed trousers with leather boots, long t-shirts and hoodies worn beneath an oversized fur coat.

DAVID BOWIE

Guardian fashion editor Jess Cartner-Morley said that 'Bowie made art out of his clothes', and he certainly pushed many boundaries with his fashion aesthetic. His androgynous appeal lasted throughout his career, but his ultimate style achievement is surely Ziggy Stardust, when his collaboration with Japanese designer Kansai Yamamoto saw the singer in kimonos and knitted unitards, and glam rock was born. Through the 1980s and 1990s jumpsuits and duster coats gave way to sharp tailoring and collaborations with designers including Alexander McQueen.

SPREADING THE WORD

Fashion relies heavily on advertising to boost its revenue. Every medium is targeted, from the pages of fashion magazines to cleverly placed, super-sized billboards and mini-feature-film adverts that air in the premium spots on television and in the cinema.

MAGAZINE ADVERTISING

March and September – the New Collections issues – are the biggest for advertising in the monthly print publications. Fashion magazines typically carry just less than half the number of editorial to advertising pages, but in practice the biggest advertisers get a lot of free, and arguably more valuable, publicity via fashion editorials. Whilst editorial independence should be carefully guarded, in reality editors and advertising directors need to keep their biggest advertisers happy with plenty of mentions outside of the paid-for ads.

Previously only high-end designers were deemed to match the profile of high-end fashion magazines, but *Vogue* and *Harper's Bazaar* now happily feature high street brands in ads as glossy as the ones belonging to their designer contemporaries.

The most expensive place in a fashion magazine to advertise is the four-page inside front cover gatefold, costing £149,010 for British *Vogue*.

AMERICAN VS BRITISH VOGUE

Pages of advertising

615 PAGES
(2015 September issue)

275 PAGES
(2016 March issue)

Average annual revenue from advertising

British *Vogue* av. **£25 MILLION**

American *Vogue* **$460 MILLION** (2013)

TELEVISION COMMERCIALS

The current record for the most expensive commercial made is the 2004 Nicole Kidman advert for Chanel No 5, which had a production cost of eighteen million pounds. Directed by Baz Luhrmann with costumes by Karl Lagerfeld, Kidman was paid two million pounds for her role in the two-minute mini-film.

THE COST OF ADVERTISING

£18,000,000
The most expensive commercial ever made – the 2004 Nicole Kidman advert for Chanel No 5.

£149,010
The most expensive place in a fashion magazine to advertise – four-page inside front cover gatefold for British *Vogue*.

$625,000
The cost per week, with a minimum four-week slot, for the most expensive billboard in the world, in Times Square, New York.

BILLBOARD ADVERTISING

High-fashion designers choose exclusive shopping destinations including London, New York, Dubai and Hong Kong for enormous and impactful advertising campaigns, featuring high-profile models and celebrities, that are almost works of art.

The most expensive billboard in the world as of 2015, was in Times Square, New York, costing advertisers a massive $625,000 (£467,000) a week for a minimum four-week slot. It is longer than a football field and offers an incredible twenty-four million pixel display for the ultimate in high-definition advertising.

Models make the most money from advertising deals with designers to be the 'face' of their products. Gisele Bündchen, face of Chanel, is the world's highest paid model with Forbes placing her top in the 2016 models rich list with a salary of $30.5 million.

HIGHEST PAID MODELS 2016

1 Gisele Bündchen

$30,500,000

2 Adriana Lima
$10,500,000

3 Karlie Kloss and Kendall Jenner
$10,000,000

4 Gigi Hadid and Rosie Huntington-Whiteley
$9,000,000

5 Cara Delevingne
£8,500,000

GOING DIGITAL

The internet has changed the way we view fashion beyond recognition, with catwalk shows live-streamed, fashion blogs reaching millions and the meteoric rise of Instagram. The glossy magazine has had to reinvent itself to stay relevant, the most successful by launching interactive online content that retains the appeal of the brand and its paper product. Other uniquely online fashion and lifestyle sites offer industry news, career listings and impressive fashion features. Visit the following sites to keep up with the fast pace of fashion.

THESTYLELINE.COM
Originally founded on Tumblr in 2011, the full digital site was launched in 2013, focusing on individual and creative style around the globe.

WWD.COM
The online site for *Women's Wear Daily* gets nearly three million monthly visitors and uploads shows, fashion features, breaking news in the industry, opinion pieces and business information.

NET-A-PORTER.COM
The online designer shopping site gets almost thirty million visitors a month and produces both free and paid-for digital content.

ELLE.COM
The glossy magazine's digital sibling is as comprehensive as you would expect, with an audience-pleasing variety of fashion and lifestyle features for over seven million visitors per month.

FASHIONWEEKONLINE.COM
With schedule listings and live-streaming of the Big Four fashion weeks, as well as listings and links to fashion weeks around the world, this is the go-to site for schedule-juggling sartorialists.

BUSINESSOFFASHION.COM
This site features news and analysis from fashion industry insiders on the business side of fashion, as well as daily digest links to other news and media sites with a focus on fashion and lifestyle.

FASHIONISTA.COM
With a monthly readership of over two million, the site caters to both industry members and consumers with tabs including business, style, shopping and careers.

REFINERY29.COM
The fashion tab of the esteemed lifestyle site, with twenty-seven million monthly visitors, is a fashion magazine in itself, full of features, fashion news, shopping and styling ideas.

WHOWHATWEAR.CO.UK
Features plenty of free content for its four million visitors on trends, news, celebrity-style, shopping and street style.

VOGUE.COM
The top fashion magazine produces country-specific daily updates including fashion and news features alongside digital editions of its print magazines.

PYLOTMAGAZINE.COM
This is the digital sister to the bi-annually published alternative fashion and photography magazine that includes art, music, interviews and features. This boundary-pushing publication makes a point of using strictly un-retouched photographs.

BAG A BARGAIN

It hasn't always been easy to get a bargain. One of the first pioneers of discount shopping was Harry Selfridge who, in 1911, opened a 'bargain basement' in his eponymous Oxford Street department store. Selfridge also defied current retailing practice by flamboyantly advertising end-of-season sales, leading to long queues outside his store. January and July sales became ubiquitous, but over the last two decades the savvy consumer sees no reason to ever buy full price and, given that the average markup on fashion items is between fifty-five and sixty-two per cent, retailers can cut prices heftily and still make a profit. There are a number of places you can find a deal, here are some of the best bargain hunting grounds.

FAST FASHION STORES
Geared up to shift stock fast and replace with new styles even faster. A recent development has seen collaborations with designers to create high fashion at high-street prices. Big players include Zara, H&M, Topshop, Primark and Forever 21.

OUTLET SHOPPING MALLS
Typically featuring designer stores offering discounts of thirty to fifty per cent (or higher). However, be aware that not all the goods on offer have seen the inside of a boutique, with some being less well-made versions specifically intended for outlet sale.

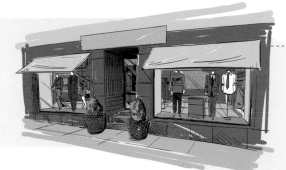

DISCOUNT BRANCHES OF BIG NAME STORES

Big name stores who have seen their profits flagging have started launching their own discount destinations, including Neiman Marcus Bargain Box, Nordstrom Rack and Macy's Backstage.

SAMPLE SALES

Once the secret of fashion editors and industry insiders, the designer sample sale, where designers sell off not only catwalk and shoot samples, but also excess from previous seasons, is now open to the public.

ONLINE DISCOUNT SHOPPING SITES

Discount sites such as *The Outnet*, the designer bargain basement belonging to Net-a-Porter, and *Yoox*, offer bargains of anything up to seventy-five per cent off. The focus is on end-of-season and previous season lines, but often ones that even fashion editors are happy to snap up.

SEASONAL SALES

The January and July sales might not be quite as longed for as before, but there are still fantastic bargains to be had, especially in reputable department stores featuring a number of concessions such as Selfridges or Bloomingdales.

DESIGNER DISCOUNT HIGH-STREET STORES

TJMaxx and it's European arm TKMaxx resell surplus designer fashion without the frills by buying up excess clothes cheaply and selling them in brightly lit stores with few sales staff.

CHAPTER 4

FASHION ERAS

With so much choice in fashion we often forget that in decades past what was considered 'fashionable' was very prescriptive; from the flappers of the twenties to the miniskirts of the sixties, every era had its own style. This chapter reveals those iconic looks and, in turn, as we look back nostalgically on the fashion of the past, charts the rise of interest in vintage clothes. It also profiles other notable influences on fashion in any given period, including stars of the silver screen and stylish members of royal families.

THE LONG AND THE SHORT OF IT

Famously, the fashionable length for women's hemlines can be used as a measure of economic prosperity. The Hemline Index suggests that hemlines rise with stock prices and, in times of economic turmoil, drop almost overnight.

INS

25
20
15
10
5

1920s

1930s

1940s

The Flapper era saw hemlines rising, finally landing on, or even above, the knee in 1926, with drop-waisted dresses ending a scandalous eighteen inches from the floor.

Recession pushed hemlines down eight or nine inches to mid-calf, but the dresses were far from austere, featuring beautiful, sinuous lines, bias-cut shapes and elegantly draped silks.

The Second World War brought cloth rationing, and make-do-and-mend became the norm. Hemlines rose not because of fashion but necessity: the material for long, elegant dresses simply wasn't there.

1950s

By the late 1940s, designers were hungry for glamour. Parisian Christian Dior created the perfect post-war 'New Look' collection, with its cloth-rich, extravagantly full skirts.

1960s

This decade brought us the miniskirt, one of the most iconic fashion trends of all time and one that stopped an incredible twenty-five inches above the ground.

1970s

From one extreme to the other, the 1970s replaced the miniskirt with the maxi as hemlines tumbled once again to sweep the floor with free and easy style.

1980s

Power dressing, oversized shoulder pads and tailoring harked back to the 1940s. Skirts were slim and short, ending at the knee and accessorised with big hair and bright red lipstick.

1990s–PRESENT

An anything-goes fashion ethos began to reign. It has become easy to wear a floor-skimming maxi skirt one day and a revealing strip of fabric the next.

In contrast to the styles that had lasted for centuries beforehand, no corset was required to give the illusion of a tiny waist because the dress fell in a straight line from chest to knee and the bust was flattened to give a boyish silhouette.

Dresses were accessorised with elbow-length gloves, a diamanté-encrusted or feathered headband and a long string of pearls. Flappers often draped themselves in a feather boa and always had a cigarette holder to hand.

The flapper dress typically had a low-scooped sleeveless neckline, dropped waist and fell to just on the knee.

FLAPPER FASHION

The 1920s marked a huge change in women's fashion: for the first time women were able to forgo their corset in favour of dropped-waisted dresses and crop their long hair into a chic bob. Hemlines rose from ankle-length to just below the knee and fashions were far more revealing of the shoulders and arms. In the United States, the jazz age had arrived and with it the freedom that gave this decade it's nickname, the 'roaring twenties'.

The fabric was typically chiffon and heavily beaded with fringing at the bottom.

DAYWEAR

Accessories were the essential cloche hat and long pearls as well as a draped fur stole or shawl according to the season.

The 1920s lady wore either a blouse, pleated skirt and wrap-around cardigan or a column dress in the same drop-waisted style of evening wear.

The art deco aesthetic of clean lines and bold prints started to take hold from the mid-1920s.

Shoes in this period typically had a buckled cross-bar and a small curved 'Louis' heel and were often adorned with diamanté.

OUTERWEAR

The word 'cloche' is taken from the French word for 'bell' and these 1920s cloche hats, typically made from felt, might be plain for daywear or adorned with jewels, embroidery, appliqué, brooches, or other art deco accents, for the evening.

The long, somewhat shapeless silhouette of the decade was enhanced by voluminous coats or capes, with wide luxuriously fur-trimmed collars and cuffs or long slim coats in art deco-style prints. For chilly evenings a fur muff might be carried to keep a lady's hands warm.

SILVER SIRENS

The 1930s saw a change in fashion: styles were more subdued than the 1920s in part thanks to the 1929 Wall Street Crash, which tempered the optimism of the roaring twenties and forced women to economise. Hemlines dropped, as they often did in times of economic crisis, and women could no longer afford to change their outfit several times a day. Nevertheless, this was the era of the silver screen, with women styling themselves in the image of Hollywood actresses like Greta Garbo and Jean Harlow.

TROUSERS

Trousers were not universally accepted for women in the 1930s, but screen icons like Katharine Hepburn and Marlene Dietrich were beginning to change that. Meanwhile, influential designer Coco Chanel maintained that if men could wear tweed trousers in the countryside, so could women. Images of the designer in wide-legged pants and a striped Breton top, or belted with blouse and pearls, did much to make it fashionable for women to wear trousers.

EVENING WEAR

Full-length and sometimes with a small train, evening gowns were made from silks and satins and cut on the bias to flattering effect. The bodice was draped and slightly full, not fitted, and the neckline was either simple or a type of halter-neck with straps hanging down over the exposed, very low-cut, scooped back. Accessories could include a small embroidered or bejewelled clutch handbag, long evening gloves, striking long art deco earrings and satin evening slippers to match the dress. Women wore their short hair set closely against their head in waves.

DAYWEAR

Everyday dresses in the 1930s fell in pleats to mid-calf, were made from light, printed fabrics, with slightly puffed sleeves that gave the shoulders a squared-off effect that accentuated the neat belted or tied waist. Smarter daywear included long pleated skirts topped with a blouse and tailored jacket or a capelet. Co-ordinating items, including hats and shoes, were key with many dress patterns coming as an ensemble.

SUITS & TAILORING

Tailoring began to make a comeback in the 1930s with square-shouldered, sometimes almost boxy, jackets sloping to a narrow waist, sometimes belted, worn with a long, straight, gently pleated skirt. A pussy-bow blouse was often worn beneath the jacket. A hat was essential and popular styles included a variation on the 1920s cloche and a small felt fedora with feather, all worn tilted over to one side.

COATS

In the 1930s coats were simply tailored for day, but for evenings women wore voluminous wrap coats with fur trims. Capes and caplets were popular, as were fur stoles.

UTILITY DRESSES

Cloth rationing, which began in 1941 and lasted until 1949, meant that dresses needed to be made with as little fabric as possible and in 1942 the first collection of 'utility dresses' was shown by designer Norman Hartnell. If you were lucky your gas mask, which had to be carried at all times, might be concealed in a cleverly designed handbag, otherwise cardboard boxes became an unwanted fashion accessory.

AUSTERITY FASHION

Fashion in the 1940s was all about 'make do and mend'. Fabric rationing due to the Second World War meant that women had to be creative with what they already had, making coats out of bedspreads and old curtains, adapting dress patterns to use a bare minimum of fabric, and painting their naked legs with gravy powder and drawing a fake 'seam' thanks to the shortage of nylon stockings.

TEA DRESSES

The dresses of the 1940s were shorter than those of the 1930s, a reaction to cloth shortages, but still had puffed sleeves and a tie belt with the pleated skirt falling to the knee. Pretty floral tea dresses made from crêpe de Chine were popular and women still accessorised with co-ordinating gloves, hat and handbag.

LAND GIRLS

Women who took over the jobs of the men in the fields who had gone off to fight typically wore labourers' dungarees but, ever determined to add a fashionable twist, land girls belted them in tightly and accessorised with a colourful printed headscarf for a surprisingly contemporary look.

NAUTICAL LOOK

A popular look in the United States at the time was nautical, with sailor suits or wide-legged trousers and a striped top for relaxed beachwear, adding a blazer for smarter occasions. The white trousers, striped top and blazer Doris Day wore in the 1948 film *Romance on the High Seas* was a major influence.

NEW LOOK

After the frugality of war-time, the arrival of Parisian designer Christian Dior's landmark post-war fashion collection came at the perfect time. The 'New Look', as it was known, used great volumes of fabric for full, longer-length skirts and matched them to sharply tailored, glamorous jackets with tiny waists. Heels were slim and high and hats were wide-brimmed and elegant.

1940S SUITS

The 1940s suit had more than a hint of things to come, with shoulders wide enough to rival those of the 1980s, a tightly nipped-in waist and a pleated skirt to the knee or just below. Wedge-heeled shoes were the perfect accessory.

NEW LOOK

The 1950s saw the revival of a truly ladylike style. After the austerity of wartime fabric rationing, the mood was ripe for fashion that splurged on reams of gorgeous textiles. Fully accessorised with hat, gloves and stockings, this look might seem formal but it can be playful too, with its overt femininity combined with plenty of sassy style.

SKIRTS & DRESSES

This was the decade of flouncy skirts and layer upon layer of net petticoat. Dresses were indulgently long and full with waists nipped in tight to emphasise the hourglass silhouette. Equally popular were slim, figure-hugging pencil skirts.

THE STILETTO

1953 saw the invention of the stiletto heel by Roger Vivier, who was working with Christian Dior at the time. The 'needle', as he nicknamed it, would be an instant hit, creating the sex symbol look of icons such as Marilyn Monroe, who is reputed to have shaved a quarter inch off one of her stilettos to force her to walk with her trademark wiggle.

HANDBAGS

Accessories in this decade included long gloves and a handbag swung artfully in the crook of your elbow, hand cocked upwards. Grace Kelly, screen icon and later Princess of Monaco, epitomised the elegant cool chic of the fifties lady and the bag created for her by Hermès – the Kelly bag – was the first 'it' bag.

STOCKINGS

A discreet flash of a silk stocking gave fifties style a seductive edge. Unfortunately this came with the hassle of suspender belts, straightening stocking seams and holding your breath to fit into a corseted waist.

BALLET FLATS

Style icons such as Audrey Hepburn preferred a simple, gamine chic – think fitted ankle-length capri pants, a classic white shirt tied at the waist, headscarf and ballet pumps – that was a refreshing alternative to the souped-up sexiness of other Hollywood stars.

BIKINI

By the late 1940s and 1950s the bikini had caught on, with every movie star worth their studio contract flaunting this risqué new style. A young Brigitte Bardot was one of the first to secure the bikini's fashion status, as well as her own stardom, using the flattering attention she received wearing it as a fledgling actress to boost her own successful career.

SWINGING SIXTIES

The 1960s started as a buttoned-up continuation of the 1950s, but within a decade fashion was unrecognisable. Women's liberation was on the agenda and many women were beginning to work outside the home. The money they earned went in no small part on the new looks of the day: tiny miniskirts, psychedelic fabrics and graphic-print minidresses matched with brightly coloured tights.

BIBA

Polish designer Barbara Hulanicki's legendary department store Biba sold fashion at affordable prices for the first time. The lavish, art deco store was inspired by Hollywood glamour, the sales staff (including a fifteen-year-old Anna Wintour) were from the same fashionable group as the shoppers and, uniquely, Biba offered a whole lifestyle to aspire to, selling not just clothes but food and household items too. Biba quickly became a hangout for the it-crowd of the day attracting film stars, models, artists and musicians.

MINISKIRTS

The new wave of supermodels, including Twiggy and Jean Shrimpton, had boyish figures very unlike the curvaceous shape that was fashionable in the 1950s, and miniskirts revealed long, skinny legs to perfection. The tiniest of the tiny was known as a 'pelmet' skirt, its width barely more than a curtain pelmet.

KNITTED & CROCHETED DRESSES

If graphic prints and bright colours were not your style, there was also a big trend for minidresses in crocheted or knitted fabrics, with patterns woven into the design.

MEN'S FASHION

In the 1960s men were given the chance to express themselves through their fashion choices: velvet jackets, military-style Carnaby Street jackets, long, shaggy fur coats and feminine clothes were worn with long hair, in a look that was shocking for its time.

SCI-FI

Influenced by films like *Barbarella* and programmes including *Star Trek*, designers such as Pierre Cardin and Paco Rabanne created collections using futuristic metallic fabrics matched with space-helmet-like hats, oversized goggles and high boots.

GEOMETRIC PRINTS & BOLD COLOURS

Queen of the graphic print was designer Mary Quant, who, by 1963, had opened two of her 'Bazaar' boutiques in London, hub of the swinging sixties. Influenced by the beatniks and the dance clothes she had worn as a child, Quant created bold black-and-white geometric prints for her bottom-skimming dresses. Her trademark Vidal Sassoon bob and brightly coloured tights finished off the look. Similarly, in 1965 Yves Saint Laurent created the Mondrian collection, including six cocktail dresses based on the colourful, graphic art of Dutch painter Piet Mondrian.

FLOWER POWER

This was the era of bell bottoms, platform heels, tank tops, hippie peace and love, big hair and disco fever – the 1970s had some challenging fashions to love. The fashion crowd took their inspiration from New York's Studio 54 and their designer of choice was Halston. Often known as the designer who invented minimalism, his draped evening gowns and trademark jersey halter-neck dresses were unforgettable in their simplicity. As much of a partygoer as the celebrities he dressed, Halston was often surrounded by the likes of Andy Warhol, Truman Capote, Elizabeth Taylor and Bianca Jagger.

DISCO

1977 released into the world the dancing phenomenon that was John Travolta in *Saturday Night Fever*, and the craze for disco took off. Bell-bottomed all-in-ones in clingy shiny materials were all the craze, with platforms to match and, for the brave, a pair of skates for the roller disco.

FLOWER POWER

Hippies reacted to the straight-laced values of previous decades. The fashion for loose kaftans, homespun tie-dye blouses and bare feet or sandals was tied closely to the peace and love message they spread, as well as emphasising personal freedom and rejecting gender stereotypes. Men as well as women wore their hair long and flowing.

THE CLOTHES THAT MADE THE SEVENTIES

BELL-BOTTOMS
Perhaps the most memorable 1970s fashion trend was for enormous flared trousers in swirling psychedelic prints, or velvet in browns, greens and purples. Popularised by Sonny and Cher on their television show and quickly picked up by mainstream designers, some were so large they were known as 'elephant bells'.

PLATFORM HEELS
Built up on both the sole and the heel, platform shoes will forever be linked to the 1970s. Made in a dizzying array of colours, prints and fabrics, there was a platform to match all outfits. Stars like Elton John in his glam-rock phase and David Bowie were big fans.

DENIM
Denim became mainstream in the 1970s, with everything from bell-bottomed flares, coats, dresses, skirts, hot pants and 'loons' – the skin-tight trousers that flared massively at the bottom – being produced in the fabric.

WRAP DRESS
In 1974 Diane Von Furstenberg created a fashion classic: the wrap dress. Made from silk jersey and cut in such as way that it flattered all women, the wrap was originally made in garish 1970s prints and was an instant classic. By 1976 the designer had sold over five million dresses, earning herself the cover of *Newsweek*.

PUNK ROCK
In stark contrast to the soft, peaceful hippie movement, the 1970s saw the rise of a musical counter-culture with an equally controversial way of dressing. Starting in New York with the bands New York Dolls, The Ramones and The Velvet Underground, punk took off simultaneously in London with Vivienne Westwood and Malcolm McLaren's King's Road punk boutique, where musicians including Adam Ant, the Sex Pistols and Siouxsie Sioux shopped for rubber, bondage gear and slogan t-shirts.

YOU'VE GOT THE LOOK

The 1980s was a decade of excess: in banking and media circles designer labels and disposable income were brashly displayed and the champagne flowed freely, but it had a lot to answer for when it came to fashion, Fanny packs (aka bum bags), ra-ra skirts, leg warmers and acid-wash denim are trends many of us would like to forget but, like it or not, the decade's iconic looks refuse to be forgotten.

POP'S INFLUENCE

Many pop stars had a big influence on 1980s fashion, including Madonna who in *Desperately Seeking Susan* gave us lace fingerless gloves, bandeau-style head wraps, studded boots and plenty of jewellery. The iconic jacket from the film sold in 2014 for $252,000. British band Bananarama gave us hair bows, pedal pushers, slogan t-shirts and big earrings and, of course, Michael Jackson's *Thriller* jacket was copied across the world.

DENIM

Eighties denim came two ways: acid-washed or ripped and customised. Jeans were pale or streaked and mottled from stone washing, often worn baggy with a big turn-up. Madonna was the queen of the ripped jeans, customised with several belts and worn over lace leggings. Denim on denim was perfectly acceptable with shirts or oversized blouson jackets teamed with matching jeans.

POWER SUITS

The 1980s was the decade of the power suit with businesswomen dressed in an inverted triangle shape created by double-breasted jackets with enormous wide shoulders and small, narrow pencil skirts. Shiny buttons, big earrings and bigger hair, stiletto heels, statement watches and gold hardware on status-affirming designer handbags completed the look. Cult shows *Dynasty* and *Dallas* proved the shoulder pad was equally at home in glamorous evening wear.

SLOGAN T-SHIRTS

Slogan t-shirts had long been used to wear your political views on your chest, but in the 1980s designer Katharine Hamnett took it to a new level saying in a 2009 *Guardian* interview: 'Slogans work on so many different levels; they're almost subliminal. They're also a way of people aligning themselves to a cause. They're tribal. Wearing one is like branding yourself.'

WORKOUT GEAR

Working out became a mainstream occupation in the 1980s thanks to Jane Fonda and others' 'feel the burn' campaigns, and the obligatory leotard, sweatband and leg warmers crossed over into everyday wear.

MEN'S FASHION

Men in this decade had style icons Don Johnson and Philip Michael Thomas from *Miami Vice* to pave their fashion path of oversized baggy suits in pastels and white. Or they could look to Gordon Gekko with his *Wall Street* braces, bright socks and statement ties.

NEON

Acid-bright colours, especially neon pink, lime green, bright yellow and orange, were a huge trend in the 1980s and were used for clothes, shoes, plastic jewellery and sunglasses.

A LIFE IN STYLE
DIANA, PRINCESS OF WALES

Princess Diana was a true icon of style with her own signature look both of its time and appropriate to her role as one of the most famous, and photographed, women in the world. From a shy nineteen-year-old nursery teacher, backlit by the sun so that her skirt became transparent, to the defiant, sexy woman in a black cocktail dress moving on to a new life without her husband, Diana didn't follow fashion, but her style was much-copied so that she became a fashion ambassador – literally in the case of her prominent support of British designers including Catherine Walker and Bruce Oldfield.

THE NEW PRINCESS

For her official engagement photograph Diana chose a demure off-the-peg blue suit with a high-collared pussy-bow blouse. Her wedding gown was a classic princess dress designed by little-known design duo David and Elizabeth Emanuel. It had bouffant sleeves, ruffs, frills, lace and a dramatic twenty-five-foot train. The ivory silk taffeta suffered on its ride to the church, the designers pictured desperately working to smooth out the creases before she walked down the aisle.

1 THE EVENING GOWN

The mid-1980s were a roll-call of glamorous evening gowns. Diana loved an asymmetric one-shoulder dress, such as the elegant gown covered in silver bugle beads by designer Hachi that she wore to the premiere of the Bond film *Octopussy* in 1983. Other gowns included a midnight blue Victor Edelstein dress in which she danced with John Travolta at a White House dinner.

DRESSED DOWN

Even when relaxing at her country retreat, Highgrove in Gloucestershire, Diana was never less than perfectly co-ordinated, choosing classic gingham cropped trousers and matching knits teamed with simple white tasselled loafers. Later, when she was campaigning abroad she often chose simple khaki trousers and crisp cotton shirts.

2 THE CLASSIC SUIT

Classic fitted suits and dresses became a mainstay of Diana's wardrobe throughout the 1990s as she pared her look down to a more sophisticated elegance and concentrated on her charity work, often simply accessorised with a string of pearls. At heart, Diana's style was a classic one, as shown by her love of neat suits with matching accessories.

3 THE MODERN LOOK

By the 1990s, extravagant gowns were replaced by shorter, simpler designs that continued to feature Diana's favourite style elements, such as the sophisticated off-the-shoulder little black dress designed by Christina Stambolian that became one of her most iconic looks. In 1991 she famously appeared on the cover of *Vogue* dressed in a simple black polo neck with a new, dramatic short haircut that was much copied.

FASHIONABLE ROYALS

Courted by fashion designers and with money to spare, royal wardrobes contain some of the most exclusive and exquisite clothing in the world. Yet royal fashionistas must rein in any penchant for the flamboyant. Royal fashion is about adhering to convention and choosing the correct outfit for each event, as well as for promoting the artistry and industry of national dressmakers.

QUEEN LETIZIA OF SPAIN
1972–
Wife of King Felipe VI of Spain, Letizia is one of the fashionable 'Euro-royals' whose outfits are constantly scrutinised. The Queen is always impeccably attired in designer dresses or tailored trouser suits.

DIANA, PRINCESS OF WALES
1961–1997
The most photographed woman in the world, like all truly fashionable women Diana had her own sense of style, which she moulded to the fashions of the day, often creating new trends in the process.

PRINCESS MARGARET, COUNTESS OF SNOWDON
1930–2002
As a keen socialite, Princess Margaret's outfits were the height of fashion. The daring princess always set her own rules, including going out without a hat in 1951 – scandalous at the time.

HER HIGHNESS SHEIKHA MOZAH BINT NASSER AL-MISSNED OF QATAR
1959–
This elegant member of the Qatar royal family is the progressive face of a very conservative regime. She is admired for combining Western clothing with traditional dress, in a way that does not offend Arab sensibilities.

QUEEN RANIA OF JORDAN
1970–
Queen Rania worked in marketing for Apple before meeting Prince Abdullah of Jordan, whom she married in 1993. Passionate and outspoken, Queen Rania proves that it is possible to be both a style icon and a committed campaigner.

CROWN PRINCESS VICTORIA OF SWEDEN
1977–
Princess Victoria is a thoroughly modern royal, who in 2010 married her former personal trainer. Her style is unfussily Scandinavian, whether in a feminine floral dress, a simple shift or a long evening gown.

PRINCESS SIRIVANNAVARI
NARIRATANA OF THAILAND
1987–
A regular at Dior, Chanel and Valentino shows, the Thai princess is also a fashion designer.

CROWN PRINCESS
MARY OF DENMARK
1972–
Often voted the 'most stylish' and compared to the Duchess of Cambridge, to whom she bears an uncanny resemblance.

WALLIS SIMPSON
1896–1986
Married to the abdicated Edward VIII, Wallis Simpson was a style icon whose couture wardrobe gives an amazing record of the fashions from the 1920s through to her death in 1986.

PRINCESS CAROLINE
OF MONACO
1957–
Daughter of Grace Kelly, and consistently voted one of the best-dressed women in the world.

PRINCESS GRACE
OF MONACO
1929– 1982
Classically beautiful, Hollywood actress Grace Kelly married Prince Rainier III in 1956 and her status as a style icon was sealed.

HRH QUEEN ELIZABETH II
1926–
The ultimate royal, Queen Elizabeth always appears immaculately dressed in perfectly accessorised, colour co-ordinated outfits.

PRINCESS MARIE-CHANTAL
OF GREECE
1968–
The American heiress married Crown Prince Pavlos in 1995. Despite her wealth and status, 'MC', as her friends call her, still designs for her own children's fashion brand.

QUEEN MÁXIMA
OF THE NETHERLANDS
1971–
Argentinian Máxima married Willem-Alexander in 2002 and became Queen Consort in 2013. True to her South American roots, she is always elegant yet unafraid to experiment with loud prints and colours.

THE DUCHESS
OF CAMBRIDGE
1982–
As wife of Prince William, Catherine's outfits are closely scrutinised and debated. She has done much to promote both British designer and high-street fashion.

The antithesis of the 1980s, grunge was dirty, messy and unkempt. Ripped, faded jeans, flannel shirts layered over old t-shirts or tied round your waist, cut-off denim shorts over tights full of holes, Doc Martens boots and beanies. A subset of grunge was the 'kinderwhore' look popularised by Courtney Love, who paired babydoll dresses with ripped tights, boots or Mary Janes, smudged, heavy make-up and messed-up hair.

SPICE THINGS UP

By the early 1990s there was a backlash against the hard-edged, brash and label-conscious fashions of the 1980s. Groomed and tailored was out and grunge, hip-hop and messy tousled hair a la Rachel in *Friends* was in. The Spice Girls were the biggest-selling girl band of all time and with them came platform heels, bra tops, gym wear as daywear and anything emblazoned with the Union Jack.

DENIM

Denim was still big in the 1990s with baggy dungarees (overalls), unflattering high-waisted 'mom' jeans, sleeveless shirts, tiny cut-off denim shorts (worn over tights in the colder months) and jackets over baggy knitwear.

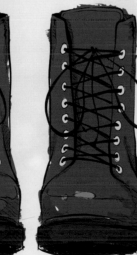

HIP HOP

The ultimate blinging street style brought to the mainstream by Will Smith in *The Fresh Prince of Bel-Air* and the rise of hip-hop artists. For men, baggy pants, hoodies, bomber jackets, baseball caps, gold chains and in-your-face colour was de rigueur. For women, pop group TLC epitomised the look with low-slung baggy jeans with men's boxer shorts peeking out, combat boots or big trainers, a crop top and plenty of metal hardware – preferably dog tags and big hoop earrings.

SUPERMODELS

The 1990s kicked off the cult of the supermodel (see pages 66–67), with the January cover of British *Vogue* featuring Cindy Crawford, Naomi Campbell, Linda Evangelista, Christy Turlington and Tatjana Patitz. The glossy beauty of the original supermodels suited the early 1990s aesthetic perfectly, but in 1993 the emergence of Kate Moss, a skinny, ethereal young girl kicked off several years of grunge fashion.

SKATER DRESSES & DOC MARTENS

Another facet to the grunge trend in the 1990s, inspired by Alicia Silverstone's Cher in *Clueless*, was the floral or plaid skater dress teamed with a cute hat and Doc Martens, or plaid skater skirt matched with a crop top.

THE NOUGHTIES

Noughties fashion is harder to define than previous decades: the internet had just arrived, tech obsession was at its peak and futuristic silver, metallic and jet black was sent down the catwalk in fashion shows that were for the first time put up online for anyone and everyone to see. But there was still plenty in the early 2000s that was a hangover from the previous decade, with hip-hop fashion, baggy tops and hoop earrings, tracksuits and crop tops still very much in vogue.

JEANS

Early 2000s jeans came two ways: bootcut or super-low-rise (think Britney Spears, jeans hanging off her hips in various dance videos), but a couple of years later it was all about distressed jeans that looked as old and worn as possible. In contrast, designer denim, for example the brands True Religion and 7 for All Mankind, were part of the growing trend for statement items and for the first time denim began to be seen as a smart option.

BOHO

An abbreviation of 'bohemian homeless', boho chic was a mash-up of hippie fashion with a bit of ethnic thrown in. Popularised by actress Sienna Miller and later Kate Moss and Mary-Kate Olsen, the look featured embroidered tops, short floaty printed dresses, cropped jackets, bare legs and cowboy boots or long gypsy skirts topped with a low-slung belt.

UGG BOOTS

An unlikely fashion success story, the shapeless twin-faced sheepskin boots that originated in Australia were huge in the noughties. In 2000, Oprah Winfrey raved about them on her show and sales sky-rocketed. Then came celebrity endorsements from actresses, 'it' girls and models who couldn't get enough of the boots' comfort factor. Once Kate Moss was pictured in a pair in 2003, their fashion credibility was sealed and according to the *Daily Mail* in 2015 UGG sales were worth a staggering £1.03 billion ($1.36 billion).

'IT' CLOTHING & ACCESSORIES

In the first half of the decade, heiress Paris Hilton embodied the glamorous, moneyed look of the new millennium, fulfilling our craving for all things celebrity, and with that came the desire to possess the accessory or item of clothing our celebrity of choice was endorsing: Louis Vuitton belts, Juicy Couture tracksuits, Prada trainers and 'it' bags. Even in casual wear, labels were huge and customers would queue up to buy the latest Abercrombie & Fitch logo sweatshirt.

FASHION ON SCREEN

Since the era of silver-screen glamour, films have influenced body shapes, hairstyles, make-up trends and, of course, fashion. Legendary costume designers during Hollywood's golden era – such as Gilbert Adrian, Edith Head and William Travilla – had as much, if not more, influence on fashion than the couture houses of Paris.

1920s

Silent movie star **Clara Bow** started a trend for bobbed hair, sailor trousers and flapper-style pleated skirts, while **Gloria Swanson**'s love of ornately embellished high-heeled shoes and glamorous furs was much imitated.

★ ★ ★ ★ ★

1930s

Marlene Dietrich became the first woman to swap an evening gown for a tuxedo, and bombshell **Jean Harlow** set a trend for the platinum bob and high, arched eyebrows. **Katharine Hepburn**'s love of menswear and wide-legged trousers influenced fashion throughout the twentieth century.

1940s

Doris Day's white trousers and striped top in Romance on the High Seas spawned a nautical trend, while **Rita Hayworth**'s black satin gown in Gilda became the ultimate seduction frock. Casablanca, with **Ingrid Bergman**, featured shift dresses, headscarves and that trench-coat.

1950s

Marilyn Monroe's iconic dresses included the pink gown from Gentlemen Prefer Blondes and the white halter neck in The Seven Year Itch. **Grace Kelly** carried a Hermès bag in To Catch a Thief and **Brigitte Bardot** appeared at the 1953 Cannes Film Festival in the risqué new bandeau bikini.

1960s

Givenchy designed **Audrey Hepburn**'s little black dress for *Breakfast at Tiffany's*, while free-spirited actress **Jane Birkin** captured the essence of the sixties with her minidresses and trademark basket. **Mia Farrow** appeared in *Rosemary's Baby* with an elfin crop.

1970s

Ali MacGraw, star of *Love Story*, inspired clothes lovers with her bohemian prints, handkerchief dresses and gladiator sandals; and **Diane Keaton** in *Annie Hall* reignited the 1930s fashion for men's clothing for women, with her baggy khaki trousers, waistcoat and tie.

★ ★ ★ ★ ★

1980s

Grace Jones starred as May Day in 1985's *A View to a Kill*, wearing slinky body-con dresses and bondage-style underwear. Meanwhile, Brat Pack icon **Molly Ringwald** set a style for millions of teenage girls in *The Breakfast Club* and *Pretty in Pink*.

1990s

Actress **Alicia Silverstone** played rich schoolgirl Cher in *Clueless*, sparking the trend for tartan, miniskirts and knee-high white socks. High-school chic has never been so stylish.

★ ★ ★ ★ ★

2000s

Sex in the City gave viewers four very different sartorial personalities to show off designer clothes and shoes in inimitable New York style. *The Devil Wears Prada* was the most expensively costumed film of all time, with designers fighting to lend clothes and accessories.

2010s

The Great Gatsby was a 1920s costume extravaganza, with designers including Marc Jacobs finding inspiration for their catwalk shows. Meanwhile, iconic TV show Gossip Girl sparked a trend in preppy plaid kilts and blazers whilst giving a nod to street style.

VINTAGE FASHION

There is a certain thrill to finding (and showing off) beautiful and original vintage finds, and many celebrities, including Alexa Chung, Kate Moss and Sarah Jessica Parker, are big fans – even paying special vintage shoppers to source the best items. If you don't have the luxury of a personal shopper, the following are some top tips to get you started.

LOOK CAREFULLY
Hold the garment up to the light and check for worn patches, missing fastenings, broken zips, mould or water marks, loose stitches or stains. Many things can be repaired, but it can be time-consuming and costly. If a dress has belt loops, it should have a belt. If not, ask for a discount. Armpits are particularly vulnerable as the acid from sweat can damage the fabric. Check the bottoms of shoes – they are often missing a heel tip – and reject stiff or overly worn leather shoes.

SMELL THE ITEM
Vintage stores are often a little musty smelling, but the garment you are interested in should not actually smell bad; if it does, remember that it might not recover, even after dry cleaning.

CHECK FOR MOTH HOLES
Check especially carefully for moth holes, which mostly affect wool or cashmere, although moth larvae also nibble at silk, cotton and fur. The chances are that the moths are long gone, but dry cleaning might still cause the garment to disintegrate as the fabric damage might not be visible to the naked eye. Washing does not kill moth eggs, but putting a garment in the freezer first will.

WHERE TO SHOP

Vintage clothes can be found in specialist stores and markets. Although also available from online sites such as eBay or Etsy, it is better to see and try on a garment, unless it is very clearly and comprehensively photographed with extensive and accurate measurements and a good returns policy. Auctions are usually for serious collectors with a lot of money, but this is not always the case.

ACCESSORISE

For the vintage lover who is unsure about going the whole vintage look, accessories – bags, belts, scarves and costume jewellery – are a brilliant way to give a modern outfit a unique twist.

TRY IT ON

Vintage clothes often fit differently. Items are usually smaller than in the equivalent modern-day size and tailored to the decade they are from. For example, 1930s clothes suit tall, slim girls as they are form-fitting and cut on the bias. Clothes from the 1940s are usually cut more generously, and 1950s clothes suit curvy, large-busted and proportionally small-waisted women. On the whole a vintage garment will read two sizes bigger than an equivalent modern one (so if you are a size 10, look for a 14). Vintage fabrics are usually less forgiving to stretch and wear so do not buy too tight.

HANDLE WITH CARE

Very fragile vintage pieces are not the best buy if you plan to wear them regularly; a collector will store clothes such as beaded evening dresses flat in acid-free paper. Dry cleaning is usually safest, but the harsh chemicals can affect less robust pieces, so gentle hand washing is an option.

CHAPTER 5

THE BODY BEAUTIFUL

In parallel with our obsession with clothes, fashion has also fostered a not-always-healthy obsession with our bodies. This chapter follows the changing shape of the supposedly perfect female form, showing that in fact body shape is as influenced by fashion as anything else; in parallel it looks at the effect of standardised sizing charts and the rise of plus-sized fashion. The trend for flaunting baby bumps is reflected in the explosion of fashionable maternity wear, and of course there are other ways in which our appearance can be manipulated in the name of fashion, from make-up and hairstyles to more permanent piercings or tattoos.

BODY BEAUTIFUL

Looking back to the bodies beautiful of the past you quickly realise how drastically different fashionable bodies have been over the centuries. From Botticelli's 'Venus' through to the big-and-proud body of modern-day pop singers and celebrities, there are usually only a few who fit the supposed 'perfect body'.

1482–1485

Botticelli's *Birth of Venus* shows an ethereal, long-haired, slim but shapely young beauty, often cited as the 'ideal female' and one who remains a muse for fashion designers today.

1600–1640

Peter Paul Rubens is renowned for his sensual depictions of voluptuous women, giving rise to the description 'Rubenesque' to describe someone amply endowed with curves.

1840–1900

Victorian women were forced into an unnatural shape with corsets pushing bosoms up and cinching waists. Huge crinoline underskirts and a bustle at the rear gave an impression of accentuated hips and bottom.

1920s

The flapper-girl figure was straight up and down. Breasts were bound close to the chest, waistlines dropped and shapely legs were revealed. The perfect female body had become part-adolescent, part-androgyny.

1930s

Shapely figures were back in vogue by the mid-1930s, when the feminine ideal was again small-waisted, but not overly so, showing gently curved hips and a round, high bosom.

1940s

During the Second World War delicate appearance was less important than strength. Icons like Rita Hayworth and Katharine Hepburn, with healthy, shapely natural figures, were seen as the ideal.

1950s

Sex symbols such as Marilyn Monroe and Jayne Mansfield, with their busty physiques, long legs and flirtatious pouts, flaunted their curves on screen and off. Stomach and thighs were soft and untoned.

1960s

Boyish, waif-like, super-skinny models such as Twiggy and Jean Shrimpton started a debate over unobtainable ideals of female beauty that continues to this day.

1970s

A long, lean, athletic figure was popular. Tanned, barely made-up, with glossy hair and fewer curves, actresses such as Farrah Fawcett were seen as the ideal woman. Models in the 1970s weighed about eight per cent less than the average woman.

1980s

The athletic, healthy and sexy look gave rise to a new generation of supermodel, including Cindy Crawford and Elle Macpherson who was known as 'The Body'. Tall, statuesque, slim but curvy, with shapely hips and long legs

1990s

Fashion idolised the waif – an androgynous, skinny ideal nicknamed 'heroin chic' that launched the career of Kate Moss, but made the gap between the normal female body and the aspirational one virtually impossible to bridge.

2000s

A return to an athletic, gym-toned supermodel with real breasts, impossibly long legs and a super-flat stomach; picture tanned Brazilian goddesses such as Gisele Bündchen.

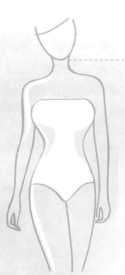

2010

The decade of the booty, with Kim Kardashian, and Nicki Minaj sparking a new plastic surgery trend – the 'butt implant'. However, high-fashion models are now approximately twenty-five per cent smaller than the normal woman. The debate between the super-curvy and super-skinny rages on, forgetting that neither shape reflects the average woman.

BARE ESSENTIALS

In 2014 the global underwear market was worth just over $110 billion (£82 billion). So-called 'Fantasy Bras' from high-fashion lingerie brand Victoria's Secret are worth staggering amounts. Yet in spite of the money spent on underwear, it is estimated that up to eighty per cent of women wear the wrong bra size. It is a good idea to be professionally measured in-store, as bra size can easily change. The steps described opposite are also a useful guide to follow when purchasing, as sizes can vary between brands.

VICTORIA'S SECRET FANTASY BRAS

$15 MILLION

Red Hot Fantasy Bra and Panties
Worn by Gisele Bündchen in 2000, it contained 1,300 gemstones including 300 carats of Thai rubies

$12.5 MILLION

Heavenly Star Fantasy Bra
Worn by Heidi Klum in 2001, with 1,200 Sri Lankan pink sapphires and a 90-carat emerald-cut diamond

Heavenly 70 Fantasy Bra
Worn by Tyra Banks in 2004 and named after its 70-carat pear-shaped diamond

Star of Victoria Fantasy Bra
Worn by Karolína Kurková in 2002, featuring 1,150 rubies, 1,600 emerald leaves

Royal Fantasy Bra
Worn by Candice Swanepoel in 2013 and covered in 4,200 precious gems and with a 52-carat pear-shaped ruby

$10 MILLION

BRA SIZING CHART

Inches	US cup size	UK	Europe	Aus	Japan
0	AA	AA	AA	AA	A
1	A	A	A	A	B
2	B	B	B	B	C
3	C	C	C	C	D
4	D	D	D	D	E
5	DD/E	DD	E	DD	F
6	DDD/F	E	F	E	G
7	DDDD/G	F	G	F	H
8	DDDDD/H	FF	H	FF	I
9	DDDDDD/I	G	J	G	J
10	J	GG	K	GG	K
11	K	H	L	H	L
12	L	HH	M	HH	M
13	M	J	N	J	N
14	N	JJ	O	JJ	O
15		K	P	K	P

HOW TO MEASURE YOUR BRA SIZE

1 Wear your best-fitting bra and pull the straps tight enough so that the bust doesn't drop.

2 Measure beneath the bust and add four inches, so thirty inches equals a band size of thirty-four inches. This system errs on the larger size and many fitters now recommend only adding two inches, so try the size down as well. If you go down a band size, you go up a cup size.

3 Measure across the fullest part of the bust and subtract your band size from this bust measurement. See chart on left for cup size equivalent.

4 When trying a new bra, fasten on the loosest hook; as the bra wears you may need to tighten it. The band should feel firm and snug, with two fingers fitting comfortably beneath the band at the back fastening.

5 Check that the central part of the bra sits flat across your sternum and that the underwire fits well directly under your bust, with no gaps or bulges.

6 Check the cup: if the breast is spilling out it is too small, if it wrinkles it is too big.

LIFE'S A BEACH

Most women can remember a time when shopping for swimwear meant an uncomfortable confrontation with a changing-room mirror bathed not in sunlight, but harsh strip lighting. But fortunately for sun-lovers everywhere, fashion has fully embraced every style of swimwear, and many can be easily bought and returned online too. So, whatever your size, shape and style - and if you aren't sure here are some tips - there is the perfect swim costume out there for soaking up some glorious rays.

BANDEAU BIKINI
Twisted top with or without straps; good for larger busts.

SWIM T-SHIRT
Not just for surfers or fair-skinned children, but anyone who burns easily or gets heat rashes.

RUFFLED BIKINI
Good for flat chests.

BOY SHORT BIKINI
Good for boyish, narrow-hipped, athletic figures.

STRING BIKINI
Best for perfect hourglass figures.

SKIRTED BOTTOM BIKINI OR SWIMSUIT
Best for pear-shaped women looking to balance a larger bottom and thighs.

CLASSIC ONE-PIECE
Good for all-over support.
Single-patterned or ruched
swimsuits disguise any
stomach rolls; contoured
panels emphasise the waist or
minimise the bottom half.

HALTER-NECK
ALL-IN-ONE
A nice vintage style that
accentuates cleavage and
minimises broad shoulders;
supportive for large busts.

HIGH-WAISTED BIKINI
Works well with a bandeau top
and covers the stomach
if you are self-conscious; good
for voluptuous figures.

TANKINI
Gives the coverage
of an all-in-one, and you have
the option of a less-clingy top.

SWIMMING DRESS
Like a sarong and swimming
costume all-in-one, these are
excellent for those who want
more coverage.

A LIFE IN STYLE MARILYN MONROE

From the beginning of her modelling career in her late teens, through her success as a Hollywood icon until her untimely death at the age of just thirty-six, Marilyn Monroe's signature style, a mixture of overt sexiness and wide-eyed blonde innocence, shone through both on screen and off, whatever her outfit.

1 GLAMOROUS GOWNS

Marilyn's signature fitted halter-neck dresses with plunging necklines, nipped in waists and full skirts or falling to the floor, were often designed for her by her long-time costume designer William Travilla, and several have attained legendary status. Many of Marilyn's gowns were so tight she had to be stitched into them, such as the nude, crystal-encrusted gown she wore to sing 'Happy Birthday' to John F. Kennedy. The dress featured more than 2,500 crystals and she was stitched in so tightly it's no wonder she was breathless during her performance. The gown later sold at auction for a record-breaking $4.8 million (£3.6 million), beating even the *Seven Year Itch* dress sold for $4.6 million (£3.4 million) in 2011.

2 TRENCH COATS

For evenings a fur stole was Marilyn's outerwear of choice, but for daytime she usually favoured a trench. She wore this either tightly belted to accentuate her waist or draped over her shoulders revealing a fitted shift dress or pencil skirt and teamed with a headscarf, sunglasses and stilettos.

PENCIL SKIRTS

When she was married to Arthur Miller and trying to cultivate a more intellectual image, Marilyn wore hip-skimming pencil skirts paired with crisp shirts, neat cashmere sweaters and stiletto heels – the perfect compromise between elegance and glamour.

3 DRESSED DOWN

Marilyn chose fitted, often cropped trousers teamed with a turtle-neck cashmere sweater in which to relax. In summer she often wore high-waisted, super-short shorts. Marilyn was one of the first women to popularise denim, saying: 'You can be feminine, even in jeans.' A very early shot of her, with her natural reddish brown hair colour, shows the actress in dark jeans and a striped t-shirt. In later years she wore a variety of styles, usually high-waisted with a belted sweater or shirt.

SWIMWEAR

Marilyn was often photographed in swimwear, both strapless one-pieces and bikinis. The style is always typical of the era, colourful or polka-dotted with high-waisted, low-cut bottoms and tops with the characteristic pointed bosom of the 1950s.

VIVE LA CURVE

In January 2017 Ashley Graham became the first plus-sized model to be featured on the cover of British *Vogue*, proclaiming her body-positive message and passion for promoting women of more realistic sizes (Graham is a US size 14, UK size 16/18). And there are plenty of other successful models shaking up the fashion industry alongside her: Candice Huffine, star of Lane Bryant's 'I'm No Angel' campaign; Precious Lee, the first black plus-size model to feature in a *Sports Illustrated* swimwear shoot; and Tess Holliday with her impressive social media following. With the average woman in the UK today a size 16 (US size 12) and in the US a size 16–18 (UK 20–22), the success of these women reflects an overdue shift towards a more realistic reflection of the many different shapes and sizes of women's bodies on the catwalk. The biggest change, however, is the undeniable demand for high-fashion clothes in larger sizes driven by the younger female shopper fed up with the limited colours, shapes and fabrics traditionally available for the larger woman.

ANNUAL REVENUE FOR PLUS-SIZED CLOTHING

High-street stores, and even designer brands, are increasingly waking up to the lucrative potential of this under-catered-for market. In the United States, spending on plus-sized clothing is projected to increase at twice the rate of any other clothing.

UK £5.08 BILLION (2017)

US $21.3 BILLION (2016)

PLUS-SIZED SHOPPERS ON THE HIGH STREET

93%
say they primarily buy clothes to hide their bodies

65%
would like to see plus-sized clothing in the same section as other sizes

90%
feel ignored by high-street fashion stores

73%
complain sizing is inconsistent across brands

81%
say they would spend more on clothing if there was more choice in their size

60%
are embarrassed to shop at separate plus-sized retailers

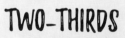

9 IN 10
women don't feel comfortable asking for help to find the right size in store

TWO-THIRDS
say plus-size ranges on the high street are poor and would rather try clothes on at home

KEY DATES IN PLUS-SIZED FASHION

1930s British plus-sized fashion store Evans founded.

1940s Women's obsession with their dress size begins with standardised clothing sizes introduced in the 1940s as a result of fabric shortages due to the war. Before then the only size given was bust measurement and women routinely sewed their own clothes or used a seamstress.

1977 Mary Duffy founds the first plus-sized model agency, 'Big Beauties' in New York.

2013 The first plus-size brand, Cabiria, shows at Mercedes-Benz Fashion week in New York.

2015 Robyn Lawley becomes the first plus-sized woman to feature in a swimwear shoot in *Sports Illustrated*. In 2016 she was joined by Ashley Graham, who was chosen for the sought-after spot of cover girl for the Swimsuit Edition.

2017 Ashley Graham is the first plus-sized *Vogue* cover girl on both the January issue of British *Vogue* and as part of the 'new norm' model shoot by American *Vogue* in March.

A NUMBERS GAME

Dress sizing was first introduced during the Industrial Revolution, when mass production created the possibility of making clothes for far greater numbers than ever before. It was not until the 1940s and 1950s that the first lists of standard sizes based on average measurements were drawn up around the world, and these have since been updated. However, the standard measurements are not compulsory and, as a result, retailers have notoriously used 'vanity sizing' to manipulate sizes to flatter their customers.

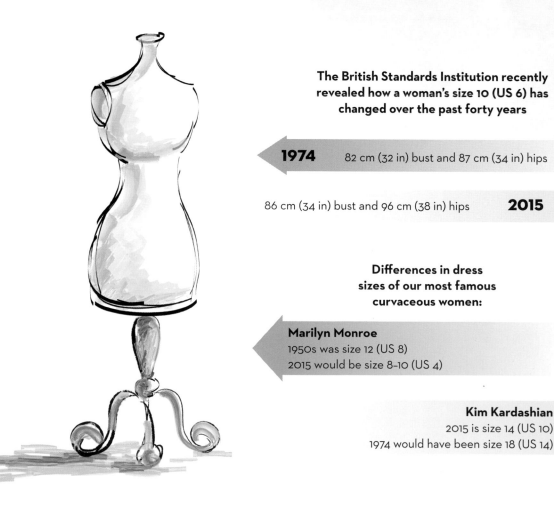

The British Standards Institution recently revealed how a woman's size 10 (US 6) has changed over the past forty years

1974   82 cm (32 in) bust and 87 cm (34 in) hips

86 cm (34 in) bust and 96 cm (38 in) hips   **2015**

Differences in dress sizes of our most famous curvaceous women:

Marilyn Monroe
1950s was size 12 (US 8)
2015 would be size 8–10 (US 4)

Kim Kardashian
2015 is size 14 (US 10)
1974 would have been size 18 (US 14)

INTERNATIONAL WOMEN'S DRESS SIZES

2	4	6	8	10	12	14	16	18	20	22	24	26
00	0	2	4	6	8	10	12	14	16	18	20	22
30	32	34	36	38	40	42	44	46	48	50	52	54
28	30	32	34	36	38	40	42	44	46	48	50	52
34	36	38	40	42	44	46	48	50	52	54	56	58
4	6	8	10	12	14	16	18	20	22	24	26	28
3	5	7	9	11	13	15	17	19	21	23	25	27

INTERNATIONAL WOMEN'S SHOE SIZES

1	3	34	34	34		21
2	4	35	35	35	3.5	22
3	5	36	36	36	4.5	23
4	6	37	37	37	5	24
5	7	38	38	38	6	25
6	8	39	39	39	7	26
7	9	40	40	40	7.5	27
8	10	41	41	41	8	28
9	11	42	42	42	8.5	29

BELLA MAMA

These days trendy maternity wear is available in fast-fashion stores and baby bumps are an accessory to flaunt, but it hasn't always been that way.

1400s –1700s

The Baroque period saw the first dedicated maternity gown. Called the 'Adrienne dress', it was voluminous and full of folds to disguise the growing bump. By the Georgian period bibs were added to these capacious dresses to allow for breastfeeding.

1800s

Victorian women hid their bumps beneath specially constructed corsets that laced at the sides rather than the back. Many women continued to lace them dangerously tight throughout pregnancy in an attempt to preserve their feminine waistlines.

1920s

The flapper era provided loose, straight-cut dresses with dropped waists that were ideal for disguising baby bumps.

1930s

Empire-line dresses were perfect for disguising bumps. But in 1938 Page Boy Maternity, a revolutionary brand launched in Dallas by the three Frankfurt sisters, finally started designing clothes specifically for pregnant women, including Elizabeth Taylor and Jackie Kennedy.

1950s

While women still didn't advertise their pregnancies loudly, it was becoming more acceptable to take pride in a growing bump and Lucille Ball in beloved US sitcom *I Love Lucy* became the first woman to show off her bump on screen, albeit wearing discreet flowing tops and wide-waisted dresses.

1960s

The fashions of the 1960s were perfect for pregnant women who could look to Jackie Kennedy for inspiration. The First Lady wore simple, elegant straight shifts and tailored jackets during her pregnancies.

1970s

Maxi dresses and baby dolls both suited expectant mothers, while the extra stretch in polyester made fashionable flared trousers and shorts a new option for mums-to-be.

1980s

Diana, Princess of Wales' pregnancy style epitomised 1980s maternity fashion, which included voluminous dresses adorned with pussy bow neck-ties and Peter Pan collars, and oversized men's-style shirt dresses. During the 1980s a number of small maternity fashion labels were launched.

1990s

In 1991 Demi Moore appeared on the cover of *Vanity Fair* heavily pregnant and completely naked. The iconic photograph by Annie Leibovitz set a trend for pregnancy photography and started the culture of celebrating a burgeoning bump.

2000s

By the turn of the century, maternity wear was becoming big business. Advances in fabric technology allowed manufactures to create forgiving clothes that grew with your bump and mainstream retailers GAP, Topshop and H&M all launched maternity lines.

TODAY

A number of labels, including New York-based Hatch and The Market and Britain's Clary and Peg are creating subtle maternity fashions that offer clothes that can transition the wearer through pregnancy and beyond, leading some fashion commentators to conclude that dedicated maternity wear may soon be a thing of the past.

MANIPULATED BODIES

There's nothing new about manipulating bodies to fit fashion. Western corsetry, Eastern foot-binding and tribal practices across the world have all altered bodies through mutilation or decoration for centuries and the modern trend for body art, piercings and more shows that humans will always want to alter their bodies. Even in the modern world the appeal of belonging to a tribe, albeit an urban one, and displaying that through body modification is obvious.

MODERN PIERCINGS, BODY ART & IMPLANTS

There are very few parts of the body that people have not tried to modify in a variety of ways; some have even gone so far as to inject dye into their eyeballs, get vampire-like dental implants, and surgical implants beneath the skin of the skull to create horn-like protrusions. These are much rarer than the popular practices of body piercing and tattoos, which have entered mainstream culture. Certain tattoo artists have even become celebrities in their own right, with long waiting lists and high-profile clientele

THE CORSET

Widely worn from the sixteenth to the twentieth centuries, corsets forced a woman's torso into a tiny-waisted hourglass shape at the cost of breaking their ribs and crushing their internal organs. While corsets went out of fashion in the early part of the twentieth century, by the end of the century a horrifying trend emerged for women to have ribs removed in order to achieve the same tiny waist, with celebrities such as Cher rumoured to have undergone the procedure.

FOOT BINDING

Beginning in China in the tenth and eleventh centuries, women's feet, especially those of the higher social classes, were cloth-bound from childhood with the goal of achieving feet just ten centimetres (three inches) long. Growing bones broke, warped and folded in on themselves, causing permanent pain, disability and even death. This barbaric practice continued until the beginning of the twentieth century.

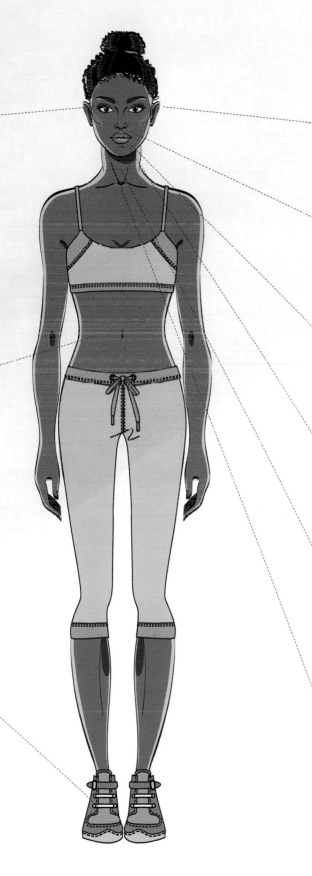

BODY MODIFICATION

EAR-STRETCHING
The Maasai of Kenya and the Huaorani of the Amazon are two of the tribes that have practised ear-lobe stretching for centuries.

NOSE PLUGS
Until 1970, women of the Indian Apatani tribe reputed to be the most beautiful, had huge plugs inserted into their nostrils and tattoos on their faces in order to protect them from neighbouring tribes.

LIP PLATES
At fifteen or sixteen years old girls in Ethiopia's Mursi tribe have their bottom lip cut and decorative plates inserted. The lip is gradually stretched, with some achieving a diameter of twelve centimetres (five inches).

TOOTH-SHARPENING
In Indonesia, the practice of chiselling teeth into sharp points is still common and women with their teeth filed in this way are considered more beautiful and of higher status than others.

NECK RINGS
The Kayan of Myanmar use neck rings from as young as two years old to gradually elongate their necks to unnatural proportions. The rings do not in fact elongate the neck, but push the collarbone down and warp the ribcage to give the illusion of a longer neck, weakening it so that the rings can never be removed.

RITUAL SCARIFICATION
Tribal tattoos, tongue-splitting and deliberately causing scars to show membership of a tribe have been practised in many places, including among New Zealand's Maori and other peoples of the Western Pacific, Papua New Guinea and Ethiopia. The practice is growing in popularity in modern societies and is seen by some as a step up from tattooing.

NAIL IT

Manicures date back to 3000 BC, when women in Egypt, India and China began to use natural dyes to tint their fingernails. But it was not until the 1930s that French company Revlon started producing mass-market nail polish in a range of colours, leading to a trend that shows no sign of slowing down.

British women spend an average of £450 a year on their nails, equating to sales of more than a million bottles a week.

Launched by *Tatler* fashion editor Thea Green in 1999, Nails Inc. started the trend for high-street nail bars. The 150 colours offered include sought-after polishes like Leather Effect.

Images Luxury Nail Lounge in Newport Beach, California, offers a $25,000 manicure that includes real diamonds and flecks of gold leaf, as much champagne as you can drink and a full-body massage.

Ellie Cosmetics' perfect wedding polish, named 'I Do', is made from platinum powder, comes in a platinum bottle, and costs around £55,000.

Rita Ora's manicure for the 2014 MTV VMAs cost a reported $56,000, her Azature Black Diamond Nail Lacquer polish containing 267 black diamonds. Azature's White Diamond is a step up even on that, containing 98 carats of white diamonds and capped with 1,400 diamonds.

The global nail polish market is anticipated to reach a value of nine billion dollars by 2020.

CROWNING GLORY

Named for the triumphant spins in the sky that returning Second World War bombers performed, the long, set and pinned curls known as 'Victory Rolls' were the iconic hairstyle of the 1940s.

Until the 1920s almost all women wore their hair long, but the Louise Brooks bob, Josephine Baker's finger curls and the Marcel wave were all popular among fashionable Bright Young Things.

1920s

1940s

ANCIENT WORLD

18TH CENTURY

1930s

1950s

Romans proved their wealth with elaborate hairstyles adorned with jewelled hair pins, pearls and beads, but Cleopatra's iconic fringed style is a myth, popularised by her portrayal in Hollywood films. In fact the Queen of Egypt shaved her head, as most Egyptian women did for cleanliness, and wore a range of wigs – pulled back braids, tight curls and her royal Egyptian headdress with a rearing metal cobra.

Softly waved hairstyles complemented the sensual fashions of the time and are forever associated with actresses including Jean Harlow, Bette Davis and Marlene Dietrich.

The 1950s offered many different hairstyles: Audrey Hepburn's gamine bob, Lucille Ball's poodle curls, a high ponytail to match your bobby socks and Bettie Page's long black fringed style that is so beloved of vintage style-lovers to this day, were all popular.

Marie Antoinette's famed hairdresser, Léonard Autié, invented the extravagant 'pouf' hairstyle that became the height of fashion. Aristocratic women competed to achieve greater and greater heights with the help of reams of gauze to hold the style together and adorned with beads, feathers and ornaments including ships and animals.

The early 1960s were all about the upswept 'beehive', but soon after Vidal Sassoon's 'five-point bob', made famous by Mary Quant and Grace Coddington, took over, and cropped styles, taken even shorter by actress Mia Farrow, became popular.

The decade of the crimping iron, perms, vibrant hair dye and plenty of product; in the 1980s women and men had no fear when it came to styling their hair.

A riot of colour, beach-ready curls, long sweep-over fringes (bangs), chunky highlights and questionable combinations like long curly locks and a dead-straight fringe, noughties hairstyles were all about experimentation.

1960s

1980s

2000s

1970s

1990s

2010s

Farrah Fawcett and Charlie's Angels were a huge influence on 1970s hairstyles, with the long feather-cut, flicked style emulated by disco divas everywhere. The full-fringed layered 'shag' cut, the wedged bob and a large afro were other popular styles.

One word: the 'Rachel'. Jennifer Aniston's hairstyle from *Friends* became an international trend despite Aniston complaining that she hated it.

Dip-dyeing first appeared in the late noughties, but the two-tone colour trend has since evolved through pink tips, a dark-roots/bleached-ends combo and into a subtler, messier, washed-out hipster vibe known as *balayage*, where colour is painted on freehand with no harsh line between dark and light.

SIGNATURE SCENTS

Perfume is as much a part of an outfit as clothes and make-up and our elusive quest for a signature scent is what drives the launch of up to a hundred new fragrances each year. But creating an iconic perfume is not easy, and renowned 'noses', experts whose sense of smell is so finely honed they can identify hundreds of individual scents blindfolded, are highly sought after. Starting with base notes to determine if a scent will be woody, rich and spicy or clean, fresh and floral, they choose from several thousand scents distilled from essential plant oils, animal products such as musk, or synthetically created, constantly testing in a process that takes many months.

'Haute Parfumerie' is the latest trend in bespoke fragrance with fashion houses including Chanel, Dior, Armani and Givenchy creating small and exclusive collections of scents and Guerlain offering a custom-made fragrance with a hefty £30,000 price tag.

CALVIN KLEIN CK ONE

The fresh and athletic 1994 scent was made iconic by its advertising campaign featuring a young Kate Moss. One of the first big-name unisex fragrances.

CHRISTIAN DIOR POISON

The brash 1980s scent is undeniably of its time. Rich, spicy and almost unbearably sweet from the heavy dose of tuberose, people either love it or hate it.

CHRISTIAN DIOR DIORISSIMO

Created in 1956, Diorissimo achieved the purest scent of lily of the valley before it had to be reformulated when some of its ingredients were deregulated.

CHANEL Nº 19

A light floral scent with notes of iris, hyacinth and lily of the valley, Chanel no 19 is a masterpiece of a clean and clear fragrance.

ROBERT PIGUET FRACAS

Beloved of Madonna and Lady Gaga, the dramatic scent has base tones of vetiver, sandalwood and musk with top notes of jasmine, violet and gardenia.

JEAN PATOU JOY

Joy was said to be the most expensive scent ever made. Reputed to contain 10,600 jasmine flowers and 336 roses, it was Jackie Kennedy's signature scent.

GUERLAIN SHALIMAR

Launched in 1925, the seductive perfume with its oriental fragrance combining iris, vanilla and rose, was re-launched in 2001 and remains popular today.

CHANEL Nº 5

Created by Ernest Beaux in 1921, the iconic scent has a sandalwood and vetiver base, mid tones of jasmine and rose and floral top notes of ylang-ylang and neroli.

FLUID FASHION

Girls dressing in boys' clothes is nothing new, but gender fluidity has becomes increasingly visible, with many designers favouring models whose appearance is not always immediately gender specific.

During the First World War, women took on men's work roles as they went off to fight, and borrowed their clothes too, as trousers for women were not yet available.

1914

Both Marlene Dietrich and Katharine Hepburn were Hollywood icons who wore masculine-style clothes. Throughout her life Hepburn made trousers and men's-style suits her trademark style.

1930s

After the ultra-feminine fashions of the 1950s, the 1960s saw a backlash against the image of the perfect demure housewife, including sexual liberation. In 1966 Yves Saint Laurent created his iconic 'Le Smoking', a tuxedo for women. Alongside women's liberation, men started growing their hair long and experimenting with more feminine clothes.

1960s

1920s

1940s

Coco Chanel revolutionised fashion by making trousers for women not only acceptable, but stylish. The designer had long borrowed the clothes of her lovers, first the French racehorse owner Étienne Balsan and later the tweed suits and trousers of the Duke of Westminster, which hugely influenced her designs.

British *Vogue* finally joined the trouser revolution by featuring their first pair of 'slacks' in 1939. During the 1940s, the Women's Land Army were issued with uniforms influencing fashion that began to espouse a military theme. The popular 'siren suits' were one such item – all-in-one jumpsuits that could be made in a variety of prints, with elasticated ankles and cuffs for warmth and a hood that was designed to be worn in an air-raid shelter.

Like Bowie before him, Prince's gender appeared fluid: he was a heterosexual yet effeminate man nevertheless possessing an undeniably sexual presence. In contrast, Grace Jones often appeared more masculine than feminine, vocally supporting androgyny and the importance of feeling both male and female.

From transvestite artist Grayson Perry accepting the 2003 Turner Prize wearing a dress, to mainstream fashion designers sending male models down the catwalk in women's clothes and the first publicly intersex model, Hanne Gaby Odiele, talking about removing stigma around those born with mixed male and female characteristics – we have come a long way from the days when it was seen as shocking for women to wear trousers.

1980s

2000–PRESENT

1970s

1990s

David Bowie was the ultimate in androgyny, spanning the gender-spectrum at a time when binary gender identity was not even talked about. Homosexuality was barely legal and yet, in clinging bodysuits with full make-up, Bowie was undeniably attractive to both sexes. His style defied convention and set a precedent that allowed men and women alike to push gender boundaries in fashion.

The grunge fashion movement saw women wearing lumberjack shirts, oversized baggy jackets and masculine boots, while public figures such as Kurt Cobain borrowed babydoll dresses and ball gowns from their partners' wardrobes. In 1998 David Beckham memorably appeared at a party wearing a sarong.

CHAPTER 6

ACCESSORIES, FOOTWEAR & JEWELLERY

Fashion is not just about clothes, there is a whole world of accessories for fashion lovers to revel in from incredible shoes and fabulously expensive designer handbags and jewellery to scarves, hats and hosiery. This chapter walks us through everything footwear related, from the handmade bespoke shoe to the ubiquitous trainer and comfortable, yet questionably stylish UGG boot. It also reveals the weird and wonderful obsessions of fashion collectors and the many ways in which those with a passion for fashion find to spend their money: designer dog accessories, anyone?

ALL TIED UP

The ultimate fashion accessory, a scarf can be an elegant printed silk square, a floaty length of summer chiffon or a woolly winter warmer. But whichever style you choose you will be part of a long and winding tradition.

It is widely believed that the Egyptian Queen Nefertiti, renowned for her beauty, wore finely woven scarves beneath her headdress.

1350 BC

This period saw the fashion for a gossamer-light scarf cascading from the tip of a tall pointed hat.

MIDDLE AGES

Hermès, the French atelier famous for its silk scarves, is founded, although it does not start producing scarves for another hundred years.

1837

Isadora Duncan, the legendary dancer who popularised long and flowing scarves, is tragically killed when one becomes caught in the wheel of her car.

1927

10AD

Romans widely adopted 'sudariums' or 'sweat cloths', which were worn knotted around the neck or waist. Fifty years later, Emperor Nero also followed this style.

1786

Napoleon Bonaparte sends his wife Josephine cashmere scarves from India.

1914

Knitting warm scarves for fighting soldiers becomes a patriotic duty.

The decade where the silk square worn as a headscarf becomes iconic, worn by trend-setters such as Audrey Hepburn and The Queen of England.

1950S

Hippies begin to use scarves as headbands and around their waists and chests in lieu of other clothing

1970S

The folded triangle shawl is replaced by the now-ubiquitous pashmina.

1990S

1930S

Rayon, a semi-synthetic fibre (see page 12), exploded in popularity during the early twentieth century. It allowed printed square scarves to be mass-produced and affordable.

1959

Grace Kelly, then Princess Grace of Monaco, wears her Hermès scarf as a sling for an injured arm during one of Aristotle Onassis' yacht parties, sealing the scarf's iconic status.

1980S

The era of power dressing begins and soon wide-shouldered sharp suits are being accessorised by large fringed shawls, with houndstooth checks being a particular favourite.

2000S

Scarves are tied every which way: draped backwards, forwards or looped through belt hoops and silk squares customised as halter-neck tops.

HATS OFF

Until the late 1950s, women wore hats every day as a matter of course; they were simply not properly dressed without one. Today, however, hats are a style choice, from the incredible creations by milliners such as Philip Treacy and Stephen Jones to hats for warmth or to protect from the sun. And, of course, hats that make a statement about your fashion identity.

TRILBY

Made famous by Dorothea Baird, who wore the hat as the lead in the 1895 stage adaptation of George du Maurier's book *Trilby*. Often mistaken for a fedora, the trilby has a sharper crown and narrower brim.

COWBOY

Invented by John B Stetson in 1865, the cowboy hat is instantly recognisable as an icon of the Wild West, and a celebrity favourite.

CLOCHE

The bell-shaped hat is strongly associated with the 1920s but has been recreated as a chic modern style.

PILLBOX

Invented in the 1930s, this small, rimless hat, likened in shape to a medicine box, became iconic in the 1950s thanks to Jackie Kennedy's love of the elegant style.

STRAW

A summer essential, there is little more stylish than an oversized, huge-brimmed straw hat and sunglasses on the beach.

BERET

The flat, round, rimless wool hat, fashionably worn pulled to one side, has its origins in the Basque regions of seventeenth-century France. Since then it has been adopted variously by the military and as a style statement.

FUR HAT

Fur has been used in millinery for centuries and the style that immediately springs to mind is the Russian 'ushanka', or trapper hat, with its ear flaps and Cossack style.

STATEMENT HATS

For parties, weddings, fashion events and catwalk shows anything goes as far as millinery is concerned, with style icons such as the late Isabella Blow never without a lobster or galleon ship atop her head.

PANAMA

Originating not in Panama but in Ecuador, this woven hat, popularised by Teddy Roosevelt and Humphrey Bogart, fell out of fashion towards the middle of the twentieth century but has been resurrected as a summer essential.

BEANIE

The classic streetwear knitted hat dates back to America in the early 1900s, 'bean' being slang for head. At first worn by blue-collar workers for its practicality in keeping heads warm and hair out of the way, in the 1990s it was taken into the mainstream and has since become a fashion essential.

FEDORA

This stylish felt wide-brimmed hat first appeared as a women's style in 1882, worn by the actress Sarah Bernhardt in the title role of the play Fédora. Its popularity grew among women's rights activists, and later men adopted the style, which is linked to prohibition gangsters in the United States.

BASEBALL CAP

The classless hat, beloved of hip-hop artists and celebrities of all types, is available in every colour, emblazoned with slogans and logos. Everyone has their own way of wearing it: brim tipped up or down, backwards or off to the side or pulled down low to meet oversized sunglasses.

IN THE BAG

There is something tantalising about a woman's handbag; its exterior is often all show, be it status-driven and glossy, brightly coloured or deliberately quirky, but the interior is different, it's contents betraying a microcosm of what is going on in the carrier's life.

Forty-two per cent of British women say that someone looking in their bag is as intrusive as reading personal emails or messages.

Eighty-two per cent believe that a woman's bag and its contents reveal a lot about her personality.

THE HERMÈS BIRKIN
Created for actress Jane Birkin in 1985 when Hermès chief executive Jean-Louis Dumas overheard her complaining she could not find a suitable leather weekend bag, the Birkin is the most exclusive, and expensive, bag in the world, a standard version retailing at over £6,000 ($8,000).

FERRAGAMO'S SOFIA
This style was inspired by Sofia Loren, a close friend of Salvatore Ferragamo.

THE GUCCI JACKIE
The classic over-the-shoulder handbag was named after Jackie Kennedy when Gucci realised the First Lady carried the bag on a regular basis.

CHRISTIAN DIOR'S LADY DIOR
Originally made by Dior in 1994 as a couture bag, it was renamed 'Lady Dior' after Princess Diana who loved the style so much.

THE HERMÈS KELLY
Grace Kelly fell in love with this bag when she used it as part of her film wardrobe and famously held it in front of her burgeoning baby bump when pregnant with her first child; Hermès renamed the bag the 'Kelly' after the actress in 1977.

LUELLA BARTLEY'S GISELE

One of the first of the series of bags named after models and celebrities, Bartley named this after Brazilian supermodel Gisele Bündchen in 2002.

THE MULBERRY ALEXA

Named after model and presenter Alexa Chung, the bag became Mulberry's best-selling style of all-time when it was launched in 2009.

THE MULBERRY DEL REY

Named after singer Lana Del Rey, like the 'Alexa' this Mulberry bag sold out instantly when the singer was pictured carrying it in 2012.

LOUIS VUITTON'S SC

Named after director Sofia Coppola who designed it in 2007 together with her friend Marc Jacobs, the then creative director of Louis Vuitton.

MARC JACOBS STAM

Named after model Jessica Stam, the quilted bag with its signature chain became the must-have accessory for 2005, but only lasted until 2013 when the designer discontinued it much to fan's dismay.

WHAT'S IN YOUR BAG?

In 2012, Cadbury surveyed British women to discover the top ten items carried in handbags, with some surprising results!

72%
Money and/or credit cards

58%
Painkillers

54%
Make-up bag

40%
Sunglasses

38%
Feminine products

33%
Diary and/or address book

20%
iPod or mp3 player

10%
Chocolate

8%
Toilet roll

4%
Underwear

A LIFE IN STYLE JACQUELINE KENNEDY ONASSIS

Jackie Kennedy Onassis is undoubtedly one of the most elegant women of the twentieth century. As first lady, wife of a Greek shipping tycoon and later as a book editor in New York, Jackie maintained her signature simple, tailored style throughout, but always managed to mould it to the fashions of the day.

WEDDING DRESS

In 1953, twenty-four-year-old Jacqueline Lee Bouvier married senator John F. Kennedy wearing a classic 1950s dress made from pink silk faille and fifty yards of ivory silk taffeta. The dress was designed by Ann Lowe, an African-American designer who made many society ladies' dresses but was little known elsewhere. Ten days before the wedding a flood destroyed the dress, which had taken two months to make, but Lowe and her seamstresses worked day and night to remake it in time for the big day.

1 TAILORED SUIT & PILLBOX HAT

The most memorable images of Jackie Kennedy as First Lady show her wearing classic one-colour tailored suits in reds, pinks, pastels and neutrals with a neat, buttoned jacket, straight knee-length skirt and matching accessories: white gloves, handbag, shoes and, of course, the trademark pillbox hat. Later, Jackie favoured classic Chanel suits in tweeds and black.

EVENING GOWNS

Givenchy designed many of Jackie's elegant strapless or column dresses, making a statement with bright colours or ornate embroidery.

2 SHIFT DRESSES

Jackie was a fan of sleeveless shift dresses throughout her life and especially in the 1950s and 1960s, when she wore a variety of printed, coloured or black-and-white knee-length dresses, all accessorised by gloves, pearls or a necklace, handbag in the crook of her arm, and oversized sunglasses.

3 VACATION WEAR

Summer for Jackie when married to JFK meant weeks at the family compound on Cape Cod. A relaxed First Lady was photographed barefoot in simple white trousers and a neat sweater, or playing tennis in shorts and a sleeveless shirt. Later, on Aristotle Onassis' luxury yacht, Jackie was more likely to be seen in a relaxed yet elegant shift, always in sunglasses and wearing a headscarf.

IF THE SHOE FITS...

Marilyn Monroe famously said, 'Give a girl the right shoes and she can conquer the world!' and women around the world surely agree. For centuries men and women have paid equal attention to what dressed their feet, both for decorative and practical reasons. But the biggest change in footwear has to be the arrival of the sports shoe and the reign of the trainer as the most popular shoe of all.

Sandals were worn by men and women, plain for men and gilded, or adorned with decorative discs, for women. A vase painting depicting Aphrodite withholding a shoe from Pan reveals the shoe's erotic associations.

18TH–19TH CENTURY

More delicate shoes appeared as Paris set the trend for satin, silk and brocade shoes with elaborate silver, gold and bronze buckles. By the nineteenth century narrow, square-toed shoes with black or white interiors, often decorated with a rosette motif, were popular for men and women.

ANCIENT WORLD

16TH CENTURY

VICTORIAN ERA

From the fifteenth to seventeenth centuries a trend took hold for a platform-heeled shoe as high as twenty inches known as a 'chopine', which elevated finely dressed ladies above filthy streets. The greater the status of the wearer the higher the platform would be.

The second half of the nineteenth century saw the popularity of sturdy, tightly laced black button boots, reflecting the strict moral values of the time. Elegant satin slippers would still be worn in the evening.

Low-heeled pumps were fashionable at the turn of the century, but during the First World War practical, sturdy boots and unattractive wide shoes were back. The 1920s, however, saw higher hemlines revealing embellished shoes with buckles, feathers, rosettes, fur, ribbons and lace.

Classic shoes such as 'Mary Janes' and laced-up brogues were popular during the war, but by the end of the decade the recognisably forties-style high-heeled, peep-toe sling back was in fashion.

The stiletto's popularity endured but was less popular among feminists, who criticised the way they objectified women – not to mention crippling them. Chunky, high-heeled boots with block heels rose higher and higher over the years to become the platform boots of the 1970s.

1900s–1920s

1940s

1960s–1970s

1930s

The 1930s saw the beginning of shoe styles we recognise today, with low-heeled court shoes, two-toned brogue-style pumps and t-bar sandals. Plain white tennis shoes appeared for outdoor leisurewear.

1950s

Court shoes, ballet pumps and strappy sandals were all popular, but it was the stiletto heel that defined fifties footwear, invented in 1953 by Roger Vivier, who collaborated with Christian Dior on his New Look collection to create the ultimate feminine shoe.

1980s–PRESENT

Spike heels were the ultimate accessory to 1980s power dressing. By the 1990s, shoe designers including Manolo Blahnik, Jimmy Choo and Christian Louboutin became household names, partly thanks to shows like *Sex and the City*. This was also the beginning of the trainer era, which continues to this day, making the sports shoe the most ubiquitous footwear of all.

HAPPY FEET

Bespoke shoes are the haute couture of footwear. Traditionally associated with men's shoes, women's bespoke shoemaking is a rising trend. While bespoke shoes for men have a higher starting price at around £2,500 ($3,300), compared to £1,500 ($2,000), women's shoes can rise to much more depending on the design. Nevertheless, die-hard fans say that once you've owned a pair you can never go back – they are uniquely fitted to your feet, have details only you have chosen and will be the most comfortable shoes you could ever own.

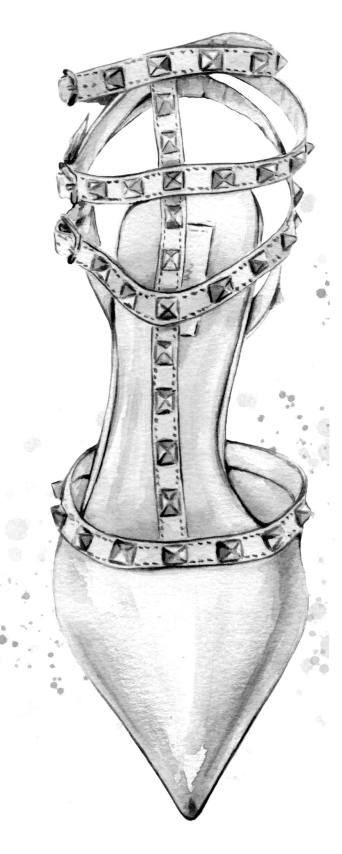

A TAILORED EXPERIENCE

 First your foot is expertly measured and assessed for shape. The last-maker will trace your foot and annotate the illustration in great detail so every part of your foot can be recreated. You will discuss the kind of shoe you want, using an in-house design as a starting point and then selecting colour, heel height and type.

Your measurements are then used to make a shoe-last, a very precise mould of your foot made from strong wood, usually hornbeam or beech.

A flat paper pattern is cut out using the three-dimensional last, a process that takes several hours to create to an individual pattern, with any detailing you want on the uppers.

The leather for the uppers is cut to the pattern, a process known as 'clicking', and then stitched together by a skilled closer.

Fitting it to the last, the shoe upper is attached to an inner sole, a manual process requiring expert hand-stitching (this is also when detailing such as brogue stitching is carried out), to create an almost-finished shoe.

About three to five months after the initial measurements, you will try on your shoes and any adjustments will be finalised before the sole is attached. The shoe will be polished and finished, the polishing process alone can take almost a day.

KEEP ON RUNNING

From humble beginnings, the egalitarian sneaker is now as at home on the catwalk and fashion front row as in the gym or on the basketball court. Lovers of the trainer will appreciate the make-up of this classic design, as well as the story of its development.

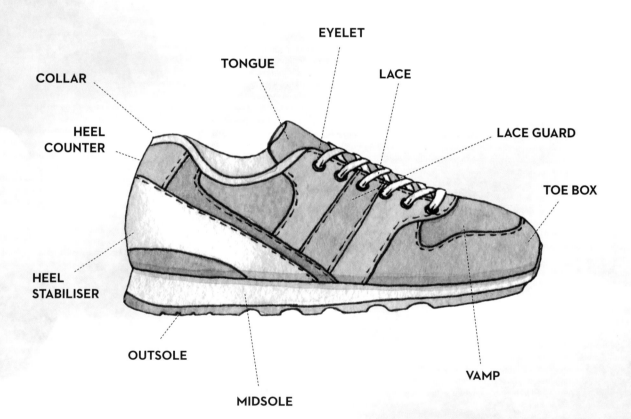

COLLAR

HEEL COUNTER

TONGUE

EYELET

LACE

LACE GUARD

TOE BOX

HEEL STABILISER

OUTSOLE

MIDSOLE

VAMP

THE SNEAKER STORY

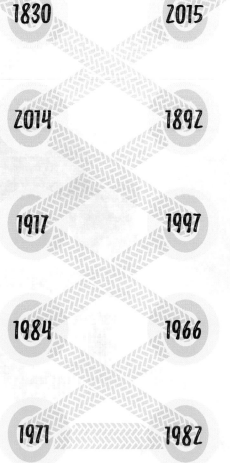

First recognisable trainer is a vulcanised Brazilian rubber overshoe.

1830

2015

Kanye West launches his Yeezy line of trainers in collaboration with Adidas.

Karl Lagerfeld sends all the models in his haute couture show down the catwalk in Chanel trainers.

2014

1892

First canvas-topped shoes, named Keds, nicknamed 'sneakers' because they were so quiet someone could sneak up on you.

The first basketball shoe – the Converse All Stars – is endorsed in 1923 by Chuck Taylor.

1917

1997

Prada includes a sneaker in its new sportswear line launch.

Michael Jordan wears Nike's Air Jordans.

1984

1966

VANS established and become a hit with skateboarders.

Adidas's tennis shoe is renamed the Stan Smith after the world number one.

1971

1982

Reebok launch 'Reebok Freestyle', the first aerobics shoe.

SNUG AS A BUG

Love them or hate them, the UGG boot – the least likely fashion item to endure – remains a firm favourite of celebrities, models (who wear them running around between castings) and actresses. One particular actress has been known to wear a pair beneath a full-skirted period costume.

THE UGG STORY

1978

Australian surfer Brian Smith heads to California, bringing with him the sheepskin boots that surfers had been wearing to keep their feet warm Down Under. Branded UGG Australia, they are an immediate hit amongst the surfing and outdoor communities, although initially limited to specialist stores.

1995

Decker Outdoor Corporation buys UGG for fifteen million dollars, as a complementary brand to its Teva sandal range.

1998

The brand has a core line of two boots, four slippers and a few other casual items; it now looks for a way to reposition itself as part of the high-end footwear market.

2000

UGG sends Oprah Winfrey a pair of 'Ultra' boots. She loves them so much that she raves about them on her show and buys 350 pairs for her production staff. Since then she has included them in her 'Favourite Things' list five times.

2003

UGG is named 'Brand of the Year' by *Footwear News* and is picked up by celebrities including Kate Moss, sparking a fashion frenzy.

2010

Jimmy Choo and UGG team up showcasing five high-end designs with studs, fringing and in leopard-skin print, costing around £495 a pair. 2011 fashion magazines and trend lists consign the UGG to the style graveyard – yet no one listens, as celebrities continue wearing the brand, happy to accept them for comfort, if not for style.

TODAY

UGG refuses to die, helped in part by the fashion revival of 'sensible' footwear, including Teva sandals and Birkenstocks. But it is the comfort factor that means the brand keeps going from strength to strength: the brand now produces not only a large range of the iconic boots, but clothes, handbags and other accessories.

TIGHT SPOT

The first 'hose', back in the Middle Ages, were stockings worn by men. Then, in 1589, William Lee invented the 'stocking frame', a machine that knitted basic woollen and later silk stockings for both sexes. During the Industrial Revolution a new version, patented by William Cotton in 1864, produced tubular cloth that was perfect for silk stockings and tights. In the 1920s and 1930s, rayon and viscose appeared as a cheaper alternative to silk, while the arrival of nylon in 1940 meant stockings no longer sagged but coated the leg perfectly. Today, a plethora of styles, fabrics, thickness, colour and patterns are available to choose from.

FISHNETS
Made from a criss-cross net fabric so that diamonds of flesh show through. Strong associations with cabaret stars, punks and 1980s Madonna.

THERMALS
Usually made from a synthetic fibre for maximum warmth, without losing the style. Perfect for cold climates.

WOOLLEN/HEAVY COTTON TIGHTS
Solid winter tights with a school-uniform feel have been reinvented by fashion designers who offer knit patterns, including argyle and ribbed.

TIGHTS BY THICKNESS

5–15 denier
Ultra-sheer nylon,
typically nude or black.

15–20 denier
The most common
weight of sheer tights.

20–40 denier
Semi-sheer, providing
better coverage.

50+ denier
Opaque tights with the
greatest durability.

TIGHTS/PANTYHOSE
Full-leg coverage to
the waist, usually made
from nylon with a gusset
either the same weight
or in a heavier cotton.

STOCKINGS
The original thigh-high
nylons worn with
a suspender belt. Silk
stockings are still made
but have no stretch and
ladder easily.

HOLD-UPS/STAY-UPS
Thigh-high, like stockings,
but with a wide elastic
silicone band around the
thighs to hold them up.

KNEE-HIGHS
Nylon knee-high
socks' that are worn
beneath trousers or
long skirts giving the
appearance of tights.

OPTICAL ILLUSION

Even those with twenty-twenty vision have realised the fashion potential of eyewear, so much so that some people now boast an 'optical wardrobe', a pair for every outfit. As a result, the total eyewear market – including frames, contact lenses and sunglasses – is exploding, with a global value of $95 billion in 2017, predicted to reach $140 billion by 2020. And yes, it is perfectly acceptable to get a pair with plain lenses! The following are some of the world's most expensive sunglasses, should you wish to invest.

$

CARTIER PANTHÈRE
With frames of 18-carat yellow gold, set with 523 brilliant-cut white and yellow diamonds, four brilliant-cut emeralds, and black spinels.

LUXURIATOR CANARY DIAMOND
Fine diamonds adorn frames plated with 18-carat gold.

BULGARI FLORA
18-carat white gold with diamonds and blue sapphires.

$59,000

$65,000

$164,000

CHOPARD BY DE RIGO VISION

Embellished with 51 river diamonds, with arms of 24-carat gold.

DOLCE & GABBANA DG2027B

The frame is gold, decorated with the brand name in diamonds.

SHIELS JEWELLERS EMERALD SUNGLASSES

Made of 18-carat gold, decorated with diamonds and with emerald lenses.

$200,000

$383,609

$400,000

CRYSTAL MAZE

Nothing says glamour like a Swarovski crystal and the brand has a long connection with the world of fashion.

Bohemian jeweller Daniel Swarovski founds his eponymous company in the small town of Wattens, in the Austrian Alps, after patenting an electric cutting machine allowing very precise cutting of crystal. His vision was 'to create a diamond for everyone'.

Marlene Dietrich appears in *Blonde Venus* wearing statement jewellery by Swarovski, her costumes adorned with crystals.

Fashion falls in love with Swarovski when designers including Christian Dior start embellishing their designs with a new Swarovski crystal that gives a shimmering rainbow effect, named the 'Aurora Borealis' after the Northern Lights. Daniel Swarovski dies aged ninety three but the family retains the business.

1895　　**1932**　　**1953**　　**1956**　　**1962**　　**1976**

By the 1950s embellishing gowns with the crystals for film costumes is commonplace, with Marilyn Monroe glittering in iconic dresses, including those she wears in *Gentlemen Prefer Blondes*.

Marilyn Monroe sings 'Happy Birthday, Mr President' wearing a skin-tight dress adorned with 2,500 Swarovski crystals. The dress sold to an anonymous bidder in 2016 for $4.8 million.

The Swarovski Crystal Society, formed in 1987 for avid collectors, is the world's largest curator society with 325,000 members in more than 125 countries.

The company's original logo, an edelweiss flower, is replaced by the iconic Swarovski swan logo.

Karlie Kloss replaces Miranda Kerr as the ambassador for the brand. The craze for the crystals continues with a wealthy Russian student covering her Mercedes in sparkle and a rocking horse covered in 82,000 Swarovski crystals going on the market for £98,400!

Swarovski stages its first catwalk show, 'Runway Rocks', featuring spectacular jewellery and one-off pieces by a range of designers.

For the seventy ninth Academy Awards ceremony, Swarovski creates a thirty-four-foot curtain adorned with more than 50,000 crystals.

1989 1999 2001 2003 2006 2007 2016 2017

Nadja Swarovski is introduced to Alexander McQueen by their mutual friend Isabella Blow and the brand starts collaborating with the up-and-coming designer, who uses the crystals in his designs to extraordinary effect. Swarovski crystals are firmly part of the fashion scene.

Hussein Chalayan uses Swarovski crystals to help create some of the dazzling effects in his 'morphing' dresses collection.

Baz Luhrmann's extravagant production of *Moulin Rouge* features millions of Swarovski crystals on its dazzling costumes.

Nike release the Air Max 97 LX Swarovski, a ladies' sports shoe in black or silver made with Swarovski's Crystal Fabric and featuring 50,000 crystals.

HIDDEN TREASURE

Pearls are an enduring symbol of style and elegance, worn for centuries by the upper classes – the Duchess of Cambridge is a fan – and made into a modern fashion statement by Coco Chanel in the 1920s. As Jackie Kennedy once said, 'Pearls are always appropriate'. They are formed when a fragment of shell or a parasite lodges itself in an oyster's body. The oyster encases the object in a crystalline substance called 'nacre', which forms into a lustrous, smooth round pearl. Cultured pearls are formed in the same way, but the irritant is purposefully introduced into the oyster.

THE MOST EXPENSIVE PEARLS IN THE WORLD

La Peregrina is the one of the most famous pearls in the world. It was made into a necklace for Elizabeth Taylor by Cartier, and sold for $11.8 million in 2011.

The Baroda Pearls sold in 2007 for $7.1 million, these pearls were once part of a seven-strand necklace belonging to the maharajas of India.

A four-strand natural coloured saltwater pearl necklace sold at Christie's in New York for $5 million in 2015.

The most valuable pearls in the world come from the Pinctada maxima oyster, native to the South Sea, twenty miles off the north-western Australian shore. The oysters can grow up to a foot wide and live for forty years, but produce just one pearl at a time. This makes them the rarest in the world, accounting for just half a per cent of pearls harvested, but their value amounts to more than thirty-five per cent of all the world's pearls.

The Duchess of Windsor's pearl necklace, which previously belonged to her mother-in-law, Queen Mary, was sold in 2007 for $4.82 million.

The Cowdray Pearls are a strand of 38 natural grey pearls with a diamond clasp that sold for $3 million in 2002.

The Pearl of Lao Tzu is the largest known natural pearl at 24 cm (9.5 in) and over 6 kg (14 lb). In 2014 it was valued at $3.5 million.

A double-stranded Cartier pearl necklace with 120 natural pearls and a 3-carat diamond clasp sold at Christie's for $3.7 million in 2012.

DIAMOND DOGS

From actress Parker Posey's infamous dog Gracie, who sits on her lap at New York Fashion Week, to pampered pups in mini-outfits designed by high-end fashion labels, dogs are definitely the ultimate accessory these days – so long as they are suitably dressed, that is.

KIEHL'S
The iconic skincare brand makes its own coat grooming shampoo, conditioner and spritz.

BARBOUR
Unsurprisingly the hunting, shooting, fishing brand has a full range of waxed jackets complete with cord collar, as well as leads in trademark plaid and quilted dog beds.

MUNGO & MAUD
Opened in 2005 in London's Belgravia, Mungo & Maud dog- and cat-outfitters catered first to posh locals before expanding globally. Renowned for their hand-stitched leather collars, dog bandanas, natural-fibre beds and blankets, and amusing accessories.

THOM BROWNE

The New York designer's cashmere dog sweaters, named for his dachshund Hector, star of his own Instagram feed, are the ultimate in canine style. Complete with the brand's signature grosgrain trim and stripes so you and your dog can have matching knitwear, the cardigans retail for a mere $590 (£440).

RALPH LAUREN

The all-American designer lifestyle brand makes raincoats, parkas, dog-sized polo-shirts and even cashmere sweaters for pampered pups. A coat will set you back around $115 (£85).

CELEBRITY PUPS

Johnny Depp and former wife Amber Heard were in big trouble for smuggling her two dogs Pistol and Boo into Australia in 2015.

Paris Hilton takes her Pomeranians, Prince Hilton and Princess Paris Junior, everywhere she goes (along with their nanny!).

Elton John and David Furnish won't travel without Arthur the cocker spaniel.

Barack Obama took Bo, his Portuguese water dog, to major events during his presidency.

Model Miranda Kerr is often spotted carrying her Yorkie, Frankie, in a specially designed shoulder bag.

LOUIS VUITTON

The Louis Vuitton dog collar and coat embellished with the iconic LV logo are perfectly complemented by the £1,700 ($2,250) dog-carrying bag.

THE GREAT OBSESSIVES

Fashion has often jokingly been called addictive, and many women (and men) repeat buy clothes or accessories they love or pride themselves on a great shoe or handbag collection, but there are a few individuals for whom collecting verges on the obsessive.

LEVIS JEANS JUNKIE

Danish denim-fanatic Kasper 'Spacey' Weinrich Schübeler has an incredible collection of Levi's jeans. It includes 20 pairs of original styles from the 1950s onwards, and every pair produced since the early 2000s, totalling around 130 pairs of the iconic brand's jeans. The collection cost him an estimated €13,000, but is worth considerably more thanks to the rarity and vintage value of some of the styles.

DESIGNER HANDBAGS

Victoria Beckham is famous for her collection of well over 100 Hermès Birkin bags, worth over £1.5 million. That is on top of her many other designer and vintage handbags, including those from her own collections. However, socialite Jamie Chua boasts an even larger collection – she reportedly owns more than 200 Birkins.

SNEAKER-HEADS

In 2013, Jordan Geller claimed the Guinness World Record for the most Nike sneakers: 2,504. This was despite Nike banning him from their stores in 2009 as he was prolifically buying from outlet stores and then selling online to build his collection. Since then, Geller has sold off the majority of his collection, keeping only the most iconic designs.

Other sneaker obsessives include actor Mark Wahlberg, who has a 137-pair collection worth more than $100,000, and rapper Drake, who in 2016 commissioned a 24-carat gold version of his OVO Air Jordan 10s, estimated to be worth two million dollars.

HOLLYWOOD OBSESSION

The biggest collection of Hollywood memorabilia was collected by actress Debbie Reynolds, and included Marilyn Monroe's subway dress from *The Seven Year Itch*. Despite trying to keep the collection together in a permanent museum, Reynolds was eventually forced to auction it in three separate auctions, the last of which raised twenty-six million dollars alone.

SHOE FANATICS

Before her death in 2013, fifty-eight-year-old Darlene Flynn held the record for owning the most number of shoes – an incredible 16,400 pairs. Imelda Marcos's collection of more than 2,700 might pale in comparison, but with most being designer labels, it is important enough as a historical record to be on display in a dedicated shoe museum.

CRAZY FOR CHANEL

Manhattan publicist Karen Oliver has collected Chanel over the past four decades, amassing a huge collection that ranges from tweed suits to accessories such as handbags, belts, scarves, perfume and make-up. She estimates her collection, which she still wears much of regularly, is worth well into six figures.

INDEX

ACKNOWLEDGEMENTS

Aurum Press would like to thank the following for supplying images:

Elliot Elam p.45tc, p.46bl & br, p.47br, pp.88–89, pp.168–169

Yoko Design 66r, p.104, p.105fr, l, r, pp.106–107, pp.114–115

Titti Lindstrem p.28, p.39l & r, p.40, p.68, p.112r, p.120, p.140, p.166

Olya Kamieshkova pp.152–153, pp.64–165

Alamy
Lordprice Collection p.108r, p.109, pp.110–111

iStock
ElenaMedvedeva pp.16–17

Shutterstock.com
A7880S pp.12–13 ; Abra Cadabraaa pp.180–181; Alenaganzhela p.44tl, tr, b, p.45tl, br; p.47tl, tc, tr, bc, p.118l; p.172; p.186; Alexey V Smirnov pp.128–129; Alicedaniel pp.130–131 Anastasiia Skliarova p.113c; Aluna1 p.15; Ana Morais p.187; Andrew Rybalko pp.82–83; Anna Ismagilova pp.160–161; Antonova Katya p.112l, p.187; Asymme3 pp.70–71; Azurhino p.15, p.52t; Babiina p.96bl; Berdsigns p.93; Biletska Iuliia p.90bl; Blue67design p.96br; Bokasana p.15; Bus109 pp.134–135; Catherine Glazkova p.119b; Chonnanit pp.12–13 Christina L p.185t, p.185c; Cincinart p.147; Claire Plumridge pp.64–65; Davor Ratkovic p.15; DeCe p.39; Designer_an p.91r; Discorat p.136; Dneprstock p.184c; Doctor Black pp.36–37, pp.66–67, p.105c, fr, pp.108–109; DoubleBubble Epine p.47bl;

Eisfrei p.138ct; ffffffly p.48; Galina Bybkina p.113t; GenerationClash p.38; GN p.90t, p.91b; Gulman Anya p.74c, p.75c; Gulnara Khadeeva pp.178–179; HikaruD88 p.45tr, p.45 bc; Iya Balushkina p.182; Iriskana p.90br; Irina_QQQ pp.116–117; Irina Violet p.137; isaxar p.55; Iya Balushkina pp.162–163; Kamieshkova pp.126–127, p.174; Katynn pp.78–79; Klerik78 pp.12–13; Konstantin Zubarev p.48; KseniyaT p.42t, p.43r; Le Panda p.52b; Lina Truman p.118c, pp.150–151; Maggical p.144; Maltiase p.48, p.187; Marina Makes pp.156–157; Michael Vigliotti p.53b; Millena p.92 Mimibubu p.45bl, p.154, pp.178–179, p.186; Moto_cat p.113b; p.139tc, bl, bc; Naddya pp.12–13; Nadiinko pp.12–13 NaDo_Krasivo p.53cl; Nancy White p.44tc, p.46bc, p.139br; Natalia Hubbert p.139tr; Neizu p.18; Oleksandr Shatokhin p.184t, p.184l, p.185b; O_vishnevska p.139tl; PYRAMIS p.119cl; Pixpenart p.48 R_lion_O p.48, pp.124–125 Ryabinina pp.170–171; Rana Hasanova p.74b, p.75t; RomanYa pp.100–101 Roman Sotola p.173; Saint A p.96c; Shafran p.57; Shekaka p.119cr; TairA pp.12–13, p.15; Tanya Kart p.113cl; Tatiana Davidova p.63; Undrey pp.174–175; VecFashion p.46t; Viktoria Gaman p.53cr; vine_suede p.53t; Vitaly Grin p.155; Wingedcats pp.88–89; Wondervendy p.91t; Yuliya Derbisheva VLG p.48

The information in this book was taken from a variety of sources both in print and online. Books used include:

Burr, Chandler *The Perfect Scent*, Picador, 2009

Hansford, Andrew, with Homer, Karen, *Dressing Marilyn*, Carlton Books, 2017
Homer, Karen, *Things a Woman Should Know About Style*, Prion Books Ltd, 2017
Homer, Karen, *A Well-Dressed Lady's Pocket Guide*, Prion Books Ltd, 2016
McDowell, Colin, *Forties Fashion and the New Look*, Bloomsbury Publishing PLC, 1997

Information was also sourced from several websites, including:
bettercotton.org
businessoffashion.com
carelabelling.co.uk
condenastinternational.com
debretts.com
ethicalfashionforum.com
fashionweekonline.com
forbes.com
huffingtonpost.com
jeansinfo.org
metmuseum.com
nytimes.com
pantone.com
reuters.com
statista.com
swarovskigroup.com
telegraph.com
theguardian.com
therichest.com
vam.ac.uk
vogue.com
wrap.org.uk

Every effort has been made to verify the accuracy of data up to the end of November 2017. Some statistics will inevitably change over time, but the publishers will be glad to rectify in future editions any omissions brought to their attention.